UE SYSTEMS

The information provided in
become familiar with the op
airliner. This manual is not intended to be used in place of any
operating manuals, checklists, or other documentation provided for
the Beech 1900D airliner.

Aviation Solutions, Dan Boedigheimer, and any and all relatives and
acquaintances assume no responsibility for injury, including death,
arising out of the use of this manual or the information contained
within.

Copyright Notice

Trademarks

Introduction

This training manual was designed to be used in conjunction with turbine transition training in a turboprop flight training device. It is based on the Beech 1900D airliner. Regardless if you actually ever fly a Beech 1900 airliner, this course and training manual will teach you the foundation you will need to take a type specific turboprop ground school.

To best prepare you for a type specific aircraft ground school, you need to become familiar with the terminology associated with turbine aircraft. The specific data and limitations in this training manual for the 1900D are important to know for the simulator portion of your training, but long term memorization is not as important as learning the fundamentals of what makes up each system. Although the make up of each system will vary from aircraft to aircraft the basic components and operating principles remain the same.

In the back of this manual is an appendix of definitions and abbreviations. Refer to these if you read any terminology or abbreviation that you are unfamiliar with.

A special thank you to Paul Skjeveland, ATP Beech 1900 check airman, and my wife Jodie for help with editing the manual.

Thank you for you purchase of this training manual. I am sure you will find it as helpful in your transition to turbine aircraft as I found my first turbine transition training class.

Fly Safe,
Dan Boedigheimer, ATP, CFI AMEI

Table of Contents

Chapter 1
1900 AIRLINER

The Beech 1900 Airliner is a twin turboprop certified to carry up to 19 passengers. Sitting over 14 feet tall and 57 feet long with a wing span exceeding 57 feet, it is the largest in the generation of King Airs.

There have been five different models of the 1900; the A, B, two versions of the C (one civilian, one military) and the D. Civilian models are identified as series UA, UB, UC, and UE. Series UD is the military version of the UC model. Manufacturing began on the A model in August 1980. At that time there were no procedures to certify a 19 passenger aircraft, so it was certified under special FAR part 41C. Today, aircraft of that size (including the D model) are certified under FAR parts 23 and 25. FAR part 41C was a short term fix to differentiate the newly created small passenger carrying turboprop from the light twin (FAR part 23). FAR part 25 requires more performance and safety features to be built into an aircraft than does FAR part 41C or part 23.

There were only six A models and 74 B models made, and by March 1991 when C model production ceased there were 174 of those. There also were six additional C models made to military specifications. Production of the D model began in January 1989 with FAA certification in 1991.

Nose Section

The nose section houses the hydraulic brake fluid reservoir,

vacuum system inlet, weather radar, and various electrical and avionics equipment. This area was designed in earlier 1900 models to be an additional baggage compartment, but most operators used the space to store the avionics and optional equipment like TCAS (Traffic Collision Avoidance System) and GPWS (Ground Proximity Warning System) which leaves no room for baggage. In the D model, this area is strictly reserved for avionics equipment.

Cockpit

The 1900 is certified for single pilot operations. However when operating under FAR part 135 or 121 a second pilot is required when there are ten or more seats installed.

The cockpit includes the six standard flight instruments on both the left and right side of the instrument panel. Between the flight instruments are the engine instruments. Replacing the standard attitude indicators and HSIs on both sides are electronic flight instrumentation system (EFIS) displays. The EFIS display for the HSI is shown in the picture to the right.

In addition to the instrument panel, there are also an overhead panel, pedestal, and side panels that contain controls. The overhead panel has switches for lights along with some electrical system gauges. The pedestal includes the autopilot controls, pressurization controls, and an auto brief system for passenger briefings. The left side panel is for the fuel controls and gauges. The right side panel is circuit breakers.

Optional equipment installed in some airplanes include TCAS, GPWS, and GPS.

Separating the cockpit from the passenger cabin can be doors that extend out from panels located behind each seat in the cockpit or a simple curtain. Since there is no emergency exit located in the cockpit there can be no type of reinforced lockable cockpit door.

Passenger Cabin

The most noticeable difference between earlier models of the 1900 and the D model is a 71" stand up cabin. The fuselage looks much taller than earlier models.

The passenger cabin can be designed to carry all cargo, all passengers, or a combination of both. For passenger carrying airline purposes there are 19 seats and a coat closet located in the cabin. There are nine rows of seats; the first eight rows have one seat on each side of the aisle, and the ninth row has three seats together in a couch formation. The seats are labeled as row 1 to 9 (front to back) and seats A, B, and C. A is on the left side while looking forward. The only seat labeled B is the middle seat in the back row. The 1900 is one of the only airliners in which 85% of the seats are both window and aisle seats. Across from the entry door is the coat closet. It allows for a total of 250 pounds of passenger or crew carry on baggage, including up to 100 pounds on a coat rack for hanging clothes.

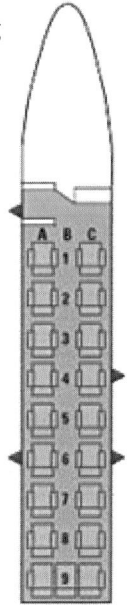

There are sixteen windows in the passenger cabin, eight on each side. Each window is made of polyvinyl butral (PVB) laminated with acrylic plastic. The aircraft may be installed with a light polarizing unit or window shades. If installed with a light polarizing unit, a knob on the window will vary the amount of shading, from clear to dark. If the windows are left in the polarized (shaded dark) position over time, the sun will deteriorate the polarization, causing a smoky film to burn into the window.

Each passenger seat has individually controlled air outlets, reading lights, and emergency oxygen masks. The air outlets and emergency oxygen masks are located on the cabin sidewall, and the reading lights are on the cabin ceiling. Also on the cabin ceiling is another set of lights that are controllable from the cockpit.

Airstair Door

The entry door doubles as a five-step stairway to the aircraft. A hydraulic damper on the door slows the rate of opening. Normal hydraulic pressure in the door cylinder is 1350 – 1450 psi when the door is open and 1000 – 1200 psi when the door is closed (with a cylinder temperature of 70° F). A plastic covered cable is used to form a hand rail and support the door in the open position. The bottom of the door is attached to the fuselage with a piano-type hinge. Four rotating camlock latches on each side of the door frame fit into posts in the fuselage and hold the door shut.

A pneumatic seal installed in the rim of the door is inflated by engine bleed air to form a pressure seal against the fuselage for flight. This system is activated by a landing gear safety switch when weight is off the landing gear.

The six lights on the entry door steps are powered from the hot battery bus, so even if the battery is off the lights can be turned on with a switch which is located on the 3rd step.

The entry door is opened by pressing the safety release button and lifting the aluminum handle upward. The door will swing out and down to form the airstair. There is a limit of 2 people on the cabin door stairway at a time.

To close the door from the inside, pull up on the support cable and hold the door in place while pulling the handle up allowing the door to close. Next, push the handle down as far as it will go until the safety button pops out and the handle is pointing down. From the outside, push up on the bottom of the door and hold the door in place while moving the handle clockwise to the horizontal position. When the cabin door is closed and locked a red [CABIN DOOR] annunciator light will extinguish.

Prior to take-off, verify the security of the door with the following checks:

1. **Handle** - Attempt to move the handle without pressing the safety button. There should be no movement.

2. **Window** - Check the observation window below the handle. The safety lock arm should be around the diaphragm shaft. Illuminated the area by pressing the red push button switch located by the window.

3. **Cams** - Check the eight observation ports located on each side of the door. The orange stripes on the camlock latches should be aligned with the black arrows.

4. **Button** - You should be able to freely press the safety button in and out.

5. **Annunciator** - The cockpit red [CABIN DOOR] annunciator should be extinguished.

Besides the safety release button, the cabin door is equipped with additional safety features. To prevent inadvertent opening of the door in flight, a pressure differential diaphragm is incorporated in the safety release button. One side of the diaphragm senses cabin pressure and the other side senses ambient air. As the differential pressure increases, the force required to press the button is also increased.

Wings

The wings are assembled in three sections, one center and two outboard wing assemblies. The center section provides the support for the engine nacelles and the outboard assemblies.

Fuel is stored in each wing. To increase the amount of fuel that can be carried, a one piece wing spar was placed through all three wing sections. The wing turning radius is 41' 2" and the tail is 39' 1". This can make it seem like if the wing can clear an object so will the tail, but in the past, this misconception has led to the wing going under an object and the tail hitting it.

Baggage Compartment

The baggage compartment is separated from the passenger cabin by a latching partition. Webbing is provided to isolate baggage between two compartments. A total of 1630 pounds can be carried in the baggage compartment; up to 1000 pounds in the forward section and 630 in the aft section. The cargo door measures 49"x 52". Lights for the baggage compartment are also powered from the hot battery bus and can be turned on with the switch located just inside the door at floor level. When the cargo door is closed and locked a red [CARGO DOOR] annunciator light will extinguish in the cockpit.

Empennage and Aft Fuselage

The aerodynamic enhancements added from the early King Air include a T-tail, stabilons, tailets, and vortex generators. The T-tail includes the vertical and horizontal stabilizer, rudder, tailets, and elevator with attached trim tabs. Because the T-tail is not disturbed by prop wash or down wash from the wings, it flies in undisturbed air. The advantages of this are lightened control forces, less metal fatigue, fewer pitch changes from a change in flaps or power settings, and a larger center of gravity range. The T-tail has enough airflow to become effective at 65 knots. De-ice boots are located on the leading edge of the horizontal stabilizer.

The small horizontal surfaces located below the T-tail and aft of the baggage door are stabilons. They are an additional wing for the aircraft and produce lift. The stabilons allow for greater pitch stability, let the aircraft climb in a stalled condition, widen the CG range, and aid in recovery from deep stalls.

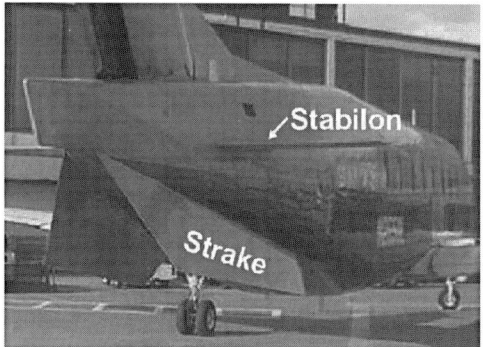
Stabilon

Strake

Located on the aft bottom of the fuselage are strakes that aid in directional stability, and help dampen any yaw movements of the tail section.

The tailets, also part of the T-tail, are the two vertical fins that extend down from the horizontal stabilizer. They aid in the directional stability at slow speeds and lower the V_{mc} speed. The leading edges of the tailets are equipped with de-ice boots.

There are two types of vortex generators on the 1900. One type is located on the leading edge of the

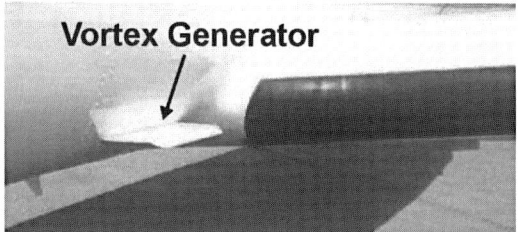
Vortex Generator

flaps, which are only visible when the flaps are extended. They add energy to the boundary layer and keep the air closer to the wing for a longer period of time, which reduces the stall speed. The other type of vortex generator lowers interference drag at the point where the wing attaches to the fuselage. It is a 4" x 10" x 1/8" thick piece of metal attached to the fuselage just forward of the wing.

There are winglets installed on the end of each wing. Winglets utilize the slipstream of air on the end of the wing to produce additional lift.

Emergency Exits

There are three emergency exit doors; two are located on the right side and one on the left of the passenger cabin. Each emergency exit has a gray stripe around it so it may be identified from the outside. The doors

are opened from the outside by a pull-out type handle located in the upper center of the door. Doors are identified from inside the aircraft as both seats in row 6 and the right side seat in row 4. To open the emergency exit from inside, pull the flush mounted handle and pull the plug-type door into the cabin. This emergency exit is not connected to the door warning circuit, so always make sure it is secure before flight. Do not try to open an emergency exit while the aircraft is pressurized.

For security when the aircraft is parked, the emergency exit doors can be locked so that they cannot be opened from the outside. The emergency exits can be locked to prevent entry into or exit from the aircraft by putting a locking pin in the hole next to the release handle.

Airspeed Limitations

Speed	KIAS	Remarks
Maneuvering V_A (16,950 LBS)	178	Do not make full or abrupt control movements above this speed.
Flap Extension V_{FE} Flaps 17° Flaps 35° (UE 1-78) (UE 79 and after)	188 143 154	Do not extend flaps or operate with flaps in prescribed position above these speeds.
Landing Gear Operating V_{LO} Extension Retraction	180 180	Do not extend or retract the landing gear above this speed.
Maximum Landing Gear Extended V_{LE}	180	Do not exceed this speed with the landing gear extended.
Minimum Control Airspeed V_{MCA} Flaps Up Flaps 17°	92 92	Lowest airspeed the airplane is directionally controllable when the critical engine is inoperative.
Maximum Operating Speed V_{MO} to 13,200 ft V_{MO} 13,200 to 25,000 ft	248 248-195	Maximum speed for any operation.

Airspeed Indicator

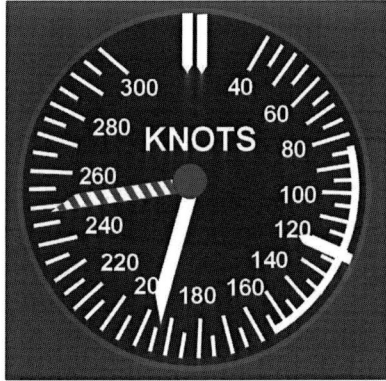

Marking	KIAS	Significance
Lower Limit of White Arc	84	V_{SO} at 16,950 with flaps 35° and idle power.
White Arc (UE 1 – 78)	84 to 143	Full-flap operating range.
White Arc (UE 79 and after)	84 to 154	Full-flap operating range.
Red and White Hash marked Pointer	248	Maximum speed for any operation sea level to 13,200 feet.
Red and White Hash marked Pointer	248 to 195	Maximum speed for any operation 13,200 feet to 25,000 feet (0.48 Mach).

Weight Limitations

Maximum Ramp Weight .... 17,230 LBS
Maximum Takeoff Weight .... 17,120 LBS
Maximum Landing Weight.. 16,765 LBS
Maximum Zero Fuel Weight .... 15,165 LBS

Maneuver Limitations

This is a normal category airplane. Acrobatic maneuvers, including spins, are prohibited.

Load Factor Limitations

With Flaps up:
      3.0 G-Positive
      1.2 G-Negative
With Flaps 17° or Flaps 35°:
      2.0 G-Positive
      0.0 G-Negative

Flight Crew Limitation

Minimum Flight Crew is one pilot unless the operation requires a copilot. (Part 135 and 121 require a copilot for operations with over 10 seats.)

Pressure Altitude Limitations

Normal .... 25,000 FT
Operation with Aviation Gasoline .... 15,000 FT

Outside Air Temperature Limitations

Sea Level to 25,000 FT Pressure Altitude .... ISA + 37° C

Chapter 2
ENGINES

In 1961, Pratt and Whitney of Canada first certified the popular PT6A line of engines. Over 40,000 of the powerplants have been delivered worldwide, and they have accumulated more than 275 million flight hours with an inflight shutdown rate of one per 333,333 hours. The Beechcraft 1900D airliner is powered by one of these models, the PT6A-67D.

PT6A-67D is an acronym defining the engine as follows:

- PT = Propeller Turbine
- 6   = 6th Propeller Turbine Design by Pratt and Whitney
- A   = Advanced
- 67D = Model number

General Engine

The engine can be defined by its major properties. The PT6A-67D can be defined as:

- reverse flow
- free turbine
- flat rated to 1279 shaft horsepower (shp)

Reverse flow indicates the direction of airflow through the engine. Air enters the engine through an inlet behind the propeller and flows to the rear of the engine. It then reverses course and flows forward to the front of the engine before it reverses again and comes out through the exhaust stacks.

The free turbine refers to the two major sections of the engine, the gas generator and power turbine sections, which rotate freely, having no physical connection between them.

Flat rated is the same as "D" rated. The engine is actually able to put out more horsepower than it is rated for. At sea level and standard temperature the engine power is limited so that as you climb or the temperatures get warmer than standard you can still achieve the "full" power the engine is rated for. Flat rating the engine also increases engine longevity.

The PT6A-67D engine is flat rated at takeoff for 1279 shaft horsepower. Shp is a measurement of propeller rpm and the torque applied to turn the propeller shaft. Another rating for a turboprop engine is equivalent shaft horsepower (eshp). Eshp equals shp plus the extra thrust produced by exhaust leaving the engine (approximately an additional 10% thrust). The PT6A-67D is rated at takeoff for 1353 eshp.

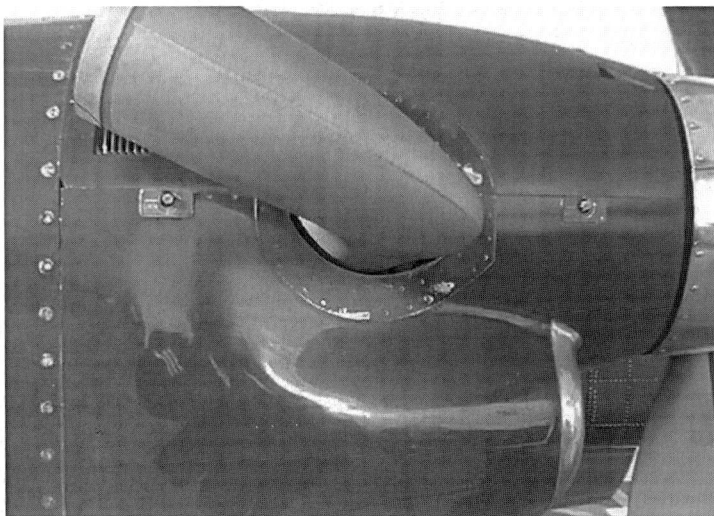

Defining Engine Locations

Engine locations, called stations, are defined by using numbers. In the PT6A-67D there are seven stations, numbered 1-7. Engine station number 1 is in the aft section of the engine and the numbers increase as you move forward. The numbers refer to specific pressure or temperature points in the engine. For example, bleed air off the engine is called P_3 air. This refers to where the air comes from, engine station number 3. The P stands for pressure, a T for temperature. Engine station number 5 is located further forward (specifically between the compressor and first stage power turbine). The T_5 station is the place Interstage Turbine Temperature (ITT) is taken.

Engine Sections

The engine can be broken down into five sections:

- Gas Generator
- Combustion
- Power

- Accessory Gearbox
- Reduction Gearbox

Gas Generator

There are two major rotating shafts in the PT6A engine, the gas generator and the power shaft. The gas generator shaft has five compressors on it. It is called a free turbine that rotates counter-clockwise and is used to compress air to 12 times its original pressure. The speed of rotation of the gas generator shaft is displayed in the cockpit on the N_1 gauge as a percentage of maximum RPM.

Air enters the engine through the air inlet located on the lower front of each engine nacelle (photo on right). Due to the reverse flow design, the air flows from the inlet to the aft portion of the engine and through an abifricated plenum (wire mesh screen).

The air then flows through five compressors; four axial flow and one centrifugal flow. An axial flow compressor compresses air in a straight line. Between each compressor is a row of stator vanes. Stator vanes are fixed position metal one inch long plates attached to the inside of the engine casing. The stator vanes raise the air's static

pressure and direct it to the next stage of compression. The centrifugal flow compressor is the last in the line and compresses the air and changes the airflow at a 90 degree angle. Instead of another row of stator vanes after the centrifugal flow compressor, the air flows through diffuser tubes which direct the airflow another 90 degrees and toward the burner can. All five of the compressors rotate on one shaft. In technical terms it is called a four stage axial flow, single stage centrifugal flow compressor driven by a single stage reaction turbine. Each axial flow compressor has its own engine station number. They are numbered 1 through 4. The centrifugal flow compressor does not have its own number. It is located between engine station number 4 and 5. Station 5 is the split between the gas generator and the power shaft.

Axial flow compressors are most efficient at low power settings. Centrifugal flow compressors are most efficient at high power settings. Because of the efficiency of the axial flow compressors at low power settings, too much air is compressed and sent toward the centrifugal flow compressor. To alleviate this pressure, air is routed from the fourth stage of compression to a compressor bleed valve at the $P_{2.5}$ section of the engine to protect from having a compressor stall. If you think of each vane on a compressor blade like an airplane wing, a compressor stall is when the airflow over the vane (wing) is disrupted and no longer producing compression (lift). The compressor bleed air valve is fully open, allowing excess pressure to escape between 0-72% N_1. The valve begins to close at 72% and is fully closed at 90% of maximum N_1. At 90% N_1 the centrifugal flow compressor is now more efficient than the axial flow compressor, and a compressor stall caused by the difference in efficiencies is no longer a concern. The excess air vented through the bleed air valve, when open, is routed back to the first stage of compression.

Combustion

The combustion section is where the compressed air meets up with fuel and a spark. This is all done in a burner can (technical name is an annular combustion chamber). The burner can is in the shape of a donut, about as wide as the engine and 3 inches thick. The air enters the burner can through hundreds of pin-sized holes. Fuel is sent via a dual fuel manifold into the burner can through 14 duplex fuel nozzles (each with a primary and secondary port) located in a ring around the outside of the burner can. During engine start, fuel is delivered through the primary ports of the nozzles until the secondary nozzles are activated at an N_1 of 40% to 45%. Secondary fuel nozzle operation can be noted by a momentary surge in fuel flow, ITT, and rapid N_1 acceleration.

Only approximately 25% of the air from the compressor section mixes with fuel to support combustion. The mixture is ignited by two spark type ignitors (located at the 4 and 9 o'clock positions). If one of the ignitors fails, the second is powerful enough to operate the entire system.

Temperature in the burner can at cruise power settings generally runs up to 720° Celsius with a limitation on start not to exceed 1000° C. There are not many metals that can withstand that type of heat, especially when you consider you are trying to conserve weight. That is where the remaining 75% of the air that does not support combustion comes in.

Consider this example. Imagine putting a candle in an empty coffee can. The flame from the candle needs oxygen to burn, so if the lid were put on the coffee can the flame would extinguish. If a hole was put in the side of the coffee can and the lid placed on it, the candle would still burn but the flame would angle toward the hole, its only source of oxygen. This creates a hot spot next to the hole in the can. Over time that area of the can will deteriorate faster than the rest of the can due to the heat. Now imagine putting hundreds of small pin sized holes all around the can. Where would the flame burn now? Yes, right in the center of the can, without creating any hot spots.

The burner can in the engine is the same as the coffee can in the example. It has hundreds of small pin-sized holes where air flows into it. The 75% of the air that does not support combustion is used to center the flame and keep the 700° C temperatures away from the metal exterior of the burner can. So what sounded like inefficiency is actually put to good use, allowing lighter weight materials to be used in the engine construction.

The ignitors are used during engine start to ignite the fuel air mixture. Once the engine starts running, it is self sustaining. The ignitors are turned off after the start sequence and the engine continues to run normally. It is standard procedure, though, to manually turn the ignitors on in turbulence or heavy precipitation to prevent a flame out from shock or water making it into the burner can.

The rapidly expanding air (coming from the controlled explosion of fuel in the burner can) flows through guide vanes which direct the air to the compressor turbine (CT wheel) located on the gas generator shaft. Approximately 60% of the energy from combustion gases is used by the compressor turbine to turn the axial and centrifugal flow compressors.

Power Section

The balance of the energy of the combustion gases that is not used by the compressor turbine to turn the gas generator shaft is used by two power turbines. The power turbines are attached to the power shaft, which drives the reduction gearbox, which in turn drives the propeller. The power turbine rotates clockwise, which is opposite of the gas generator section that rotates counter-clockwise. No moving parts are connected between the two sections. This is why they call it a free turbine design. The reason for the counter-rotating shafts is to reduce engine vibration and noise, and counteract torque.

The fact that only 40% of the energy of the air coming out of the combustion chamber is used to turn the propeller is not an inefficiency. The remaining 60% of the energy is used by the gas generator shaft to create a self-sustaining cycle to keep the engine running. When the engine is being started, there is little airflow going through it. As 60% of the energy of this airflow gets used by the compressor turbine it begins to turn the five compressors on the gas generator shaft faster. As the five compressors start turning faster, they compress more air. As more air gets compressed, the compressor turbine uses more energy to turn the five compressors even faster. The cycle continues and continues, so the more air the compressor turbine uses, the more air the compressors have to compress.

To control the cycle of compressing air to maintain the engine speed you want, the power levers meter fuel to the burner can through the use of a governor. The fuel flow governor has many of the same properties of a basic propeller governor. (See appendix A for a review of governor operation.) If the gas generator section starts to run faster than you have selected with the power lever, the pilot valve raises, decreasing the fuel flow to the burner can. Less fuel = less combustion = slower gas generator speed.

Therefore, what appeared to be major inefficiencies with the engine really are important parts of their operation. The only real inefficiency the engine has is it loses 3.6% of its energy having the reverse flow design and the engine split at the T_5 station. The reverse flow design does decrease the overall engine size and weight, and the engine split reduces maintenance costs; so it is a trade off.

Accessory Gearbox

Much like the alternator on your car is run by a belt driven by the engine, the PT6A engine uses engine power to run the generators and other accessories. Attached at the aft end of the gas generator shaft is a series of reduction gearboxes, called the accessory gearbox, that powers each accessory item on the engine. The accessory gearbox runs the following items:

- Starter/generator
- Exciter box (powers the Ignitors)
- Fuel control unit
- Two engine driven fuel boost pumps (one rated at 45 psi the other rated from 800-1000 psi)
- Lubricating oil pump
- Four scavenge oil pumps
- Air conditioner compressor (vapor cycle system) (right engine only)
- N_1 (compressor turbine speed) tachometer.

Also located in the accessory section are the oil to fuel heat exchanger and oil dipstick.

Reduction Gearbox

The reduction gearbox takes high speed, low torque energy and converts it to low speed, high torque energy for the propeller. It gears down the power turbine at a 17.6:1 ratio. When the propeller is rotating at 1700 rpm, the power section is rotating at 29,920 rpm. In addition to turning the propeller, the reduction gearbox drives the N_2 (propeller speed) tachometer, the primary propeller governor, overspeed governor, and fuel topping governor.

Engine Controls

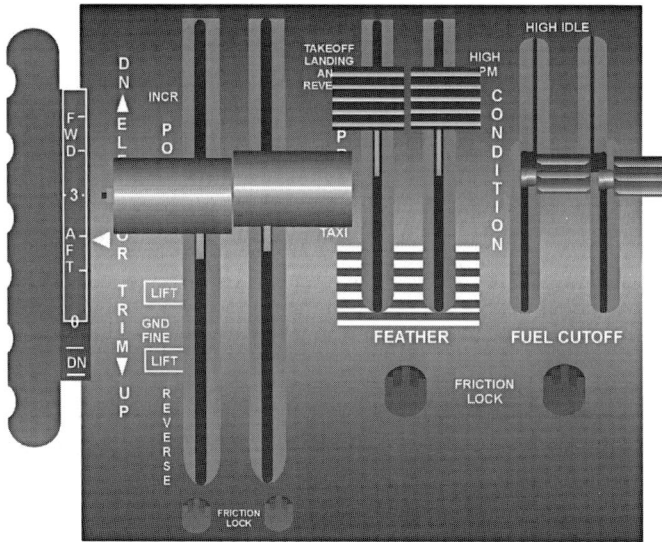

Power Levers

The power levers are much like the throttles in any piston airplane. As the power levers are pushed forward from the idle position N_1 increases applying power to the propeller. The power levers are used to control N_1. In the PT6A engine this is accomplished by using an N_1 governor (works on the same principal as a propeller governor) in the fuel control unit to regulate fuel to the burner can. In addition to controlling power from idle to maximum (called the "flight" range) the power levers are also used to control beta and reverse range. With the power levers at the idle stop, you can lift them over a detent and control power in the beta range. In beta range, the power levers control propeller blade angle only, not engine power. The beta range is used for taxi to reduce the need for braking. The bottom of the beta range is called ground fine. When the power levers reach ground fine there is a second detent you can lift them over, which brings the power levers into the reverse range. In reverse, the power levers control both blade angle and engine power for reverse thrust. Do not move power levers into the reverse range when the engines are not running because this stretches the cable.

Propeller Levers

If the power levers control the propeller in the beta and reverse range, why are there propeller levers? The propeller levers control the pitch of the propeller while the power levers are in the flight range and can also be used to feather a propeller. There is also a taxi detent position, located forward of the feather position. The propellers should be in the taxi detent position for all ground operations. Each propeller lever moves a pilot valve inside a primary governor, allowing oil flow to increase or decrease propeller rpm.

Normal propeller rpm range ground taxi operations is between 950-1250. Operation between 400-950 rpm and 1250-1395 rpm on the ground is not allowed and is indicated by red arcs on the propeller rpm gauge.

Condition Levers

The condition levers are like a mixture control in that when brought back into the cutoff position they will stop fuel flow to the engine. Unlike a mixture control, the condition levers are used to set the idle stop for the engine. In the low idle position, N_1 is 67 to 69%; in the high idle position, N_1 is 70 to 72%. The high idle speed provides more engine power for taxi without having to move the power levers. It also gives you increased generator power for high electrical loads during ground operations.

Engine Instruments

In addition to having engine instruments monitoring propeller rpm, oil pressure and temperature turboprop engines also have gauges to monitor Interstage Turbine Temperature (ITT), torque, and gas generator rpm (N_1). The engine gauges have markings to indicate some of the limitations associated with each parameter, but not all of them. At the end of the engine instruments section is a chart showing all the limitations for each operating condition; start, idle, takeoff, max continuous, cruise climb and max cruise, max reverse, and transient.

In aircraft with serial number UE-93 and after require 28 volt DC power along with whatever their input power is to operate. Some gauges in aircraft prior to UE-93 were self generated like the propeller and ITT gauge and did not require electrical power to operate.

ITT and torque meters are the two primary engine gauges that limit the amount of power that is available. They are both affected by temperature and altitude. In cold temperature or low altitudes, torque limits maximum power. When the ambient temperature is hot or when operating at high altitude, ITT limits maximum power. Which condition reaches its limit first determines the maximum amount of power available.

ITT Gauge

Interstage Turbine Temperature (ITT) is one of the two engine parameters that limit the maximum power available. When outside temperatures are warm or when operating at higher altitudes, ITT becomes the limiting factor for engine power. The ITT gauge is self- generated (no electrical power to run) and monitors interstage turbine temperature. The temperature is indicated in degrees Celsius. The green arc is between 400° C and 780° C, with a yellow caution arc between 780°C and 800°C and a red line at 800°C. A dashed red radial at 1000° C indicates the maximum limit for engine start. The temperature is measured by 8 or 10 probes wired in parallel that are located around the engine station 5. There is a 28 volt DC power back up for this gauge. Beginning with airplanes serial number UE-93 and after, the gauge's primary power source is from a 28 volt DC electrical signal from the thermocouple probes.

Torque Meter

The torque meter is the second of the two engine parameters that limit maximum amount of power available. When outside temperatures are cool and when operating at lower altitudes, torque becomes the limiting factor. The torque meter is powered by a 26 volt AC (UE-92 and prior) and indicates engine torque, in foot pounds, by measuring rotational force applied to the propeller shaft. It has a green arc from 0 to 3750 foot pounds, and a yellow arc from 3750 to 3950. Operation in the yellow arc is limited to 5 minutes. At low power settings there is not enough oil pressure to hold the servo piston steady, so there will be fluctuations in the gauge until there is enough pressure to get an accurate indication. In airplanes with serial number UE-93 and after, the torque meter is powered by a 28 volt DC motor.

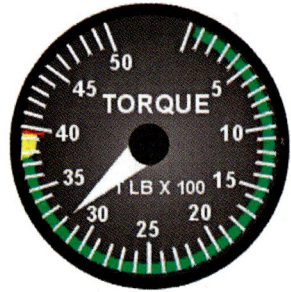

Propeller Tachometer

The propeller tachometer indicates the propeller rpm. It is powered by 28 volt

ENGINES

DC from the triple fed bus and takes input from the N_2 tach generator located at the two o'clock position on the reduction gearbox. There are two green arcs, the first at 950-1250 rpm and the second at 1395-1700 rpm. There are also two red arcs, one from 400-950 rpm and the second from 1250-1395 rpm. Operation in the red arc is prohibited on the ground.

Gas Generator (N_1) Tachometer

The gas generator (N_1) tachometer is powered from a 28 volt DC signal from the N_1 tach generator on the accessory section of the engine and measures rotational speed of the compressor shaft, in percent rpm, based on 37,468 rpm as 100 percent. The instrument has a green arc from 65% to 104% with a red line at 104% that indicates the maximum speed of 39,000 rpm. The reason you can achieve over 100% top speed is because of the technological improvements that have been designed into the late model PT6A engines. The original PT6A engine has a maximum gas generator speed of 100%. Instead of re-certifying a new engine, Pratt and Whitney decided to increase the maximum percentage. The display combines a digital read-out with the analog gauge. The maximum N_1 speed in reverse is 85% N_1 ± 3%.

Fuel Flow Gauge

The fuel flow gauge is 28 volt DC powered and indicates fuel flow to the engine calibrated in hundreds of pounds per hour. There are no limitation markings on this instrument.

Oil Pressure and Oil Temperature Gauge

The oil pressure and temperature gauge is 28 volt DC powered. Oil pressure is indicated on the right side. A red line at 60 psi indicates the minimum pressure, yellow arc from 60 to 90 psi is the caution range, green arc from 90 psi to 135 psi indicates normal operating range, and a second red line at 200 psi indicates maximum pressure.

On airplanes serial number UE-93 and after the oil pressure gauge has the second red line at 135 psi to note maximum operating range, and a red diamond at 200 psi to indicate maximum pressure.

Oil temperature is indicated on the left side in degrees Celsius. A green arc from 10° C to 105° C is the normal operating range, yellow arc from 105° to 110° C is the caution range, and a red line at 110° C is the maximum temperature.

Engine Operating Limitations

Operating Condition	SHP	Torque FT-LBS (1)	Max Observed ITT°C	N_1 % RPM	
Starting	---	---	1000 (5)	---	---
Idle	---	---	750	22,500	65 (min)
Takeoff (8)	1279	3950	800	39,000	104
Max. Cont	1214	3750	780	39,000	104
Cruise Climb and Max. Cruise	1106	3750 (6)	760	39,000	104
Max. Reverse	900	---	760	---	---
Transient	---	5000 (7)	870 (7)	39,000	104

Operating Condition	Prop RPM N_2	Oil Pressure PSI (2)	Oil Temp. °C (3) (4)
Starting	---	0 - 200	-40 (min.)
Idle	950 (min)	60 (min)	-40 to 110
Takeoff (9)	1700 (9)	90 to 135	10 to 110
Max. Cont	1700 (9)	90 to 135	10 to 105
Cruise Climb and Max. Cruise	1700 (9)	90 - 135	10 to 105
Max. Reverse	1650	90 - 135	10 to 105
Transient	1870 (7)	40 - 200	-40 to 110

Footnotes:

1. Torque limit applies within range of 1000-1700 propeller RPM (N_2). Below 1000 rpm, torque is limited to 2000 ft-lbs.

2. When gas generator speeds are above 27,000 RPM (72% N_1) normal oil pressure is 90 to 135 psi. With engine torque below 3000 ft-lbs, minimum oil pressure is 85 psig at normal oil temperature (60 to 70° C). Oil pressure under 90 psi is undesirable; it should be tolerated only for the completion of the flight, and then only at a reduced power setting not exceeding 2000 ft-lbs torque. Oil pressure below 60 psi is unsafe; it requires that either the engine be shut down, or that a landing be made at the nearset suitable airport, using minimum power required to sustain flight. Fluctuations of plus or minus 10 psi are acceptable.

3. A minimum oil temperature of 55°C is recommended for fuel heater operation at take-off power.

4. Oil temperature limits are -40°C to 105°C. However, temperatures of up to 110°C are permitted for a maximum time of 10 minutes.

5. These values are time limited to 5 seconds.

6. Cruise torque values vary with altitude and temperature.

7. These values are time limited to 20 seconds.

8. Takeoff power is time limited to 5 minutes.

9. Maximum propeller speeds vary with oil temperature. With cold oil the maximum limit of 1700 rpm may be exceeded with the propeller levers full forward. Propeller speeds up to 1735 rpm are allowed for 5 minutes so the 1700 rpm limit can be set using the propeller levers.

Engine Oil System

The engine oil system is a 15.6 quart system with only 14.1 quarts drainable from the tank. Engine oil cools and lubricates the engine and is also used to regulate the pitch of the propeller in the propeller governor and the engine torque sensing system.

Normal oil pressure is 90 to 135 psi. Should the system detect oil pressure below 60 psi, a [L or R OIL PRES] annunciator will illuminate in the cockpit. Consult the emergency procedures section of your checklist, but normally if the oil pressure gauge confirms the low pressure it recommends shutting down the engine or operating that engine at the minimum power setting and land at the nearest suitable airport.

The maximum oil consumption is one quart per ten hours. The dipstick indicates the top 5 quarts in the system, and turbine engines tend to run at a normal level of one to two quarts low. If oil is added over that set level the engine blows it overboard on the first flight. An indication of 4 quarts low is the low end of the oil quantity operating range for flight.

The oil cooler is located below the engine air inlet and is used to keep engine oil temperature at 71°C. The flow of oil through the cooler is controlled by a thermostatically operated valve. There is a bypass valve to ensure oil flow if the cooler becomes clogged.

Part of the preflight checklist is to check the oil. However, the most accurate time to check the oil is within 10 minutes after engine shutdown. To increase the accuracy of the preflight check you can motor the engine without starting it before checking the oil.

Fuel Control Unit

The fuel control unit sets engine power by regulating fuel flow to the burner can. It takes input from the power and condition levers, current gas generator speed, and propeller rpm.

There is a fuel governor in the fuel control unit that operates like a propeller governor but governs fuel instead of oil. The speed of the gas generator shaft (N_1) runs the flyweights inside the governor. The speeder spring, which provides the tension to the flyweights, is controlled by the power and condition levers. (For a more detailed discussion of a governor see Appendix A.)

If the engine is running slower than selected by the power levers (flyweights are rotating in) more fuel is sent to the burner can which creates a larger controlled explosion. As airflow increases over the compressor turbine, it turns the gas generator section faster, which compresses more air, and in turn runs the power turbine faster. If the engine is running faster than selected (or the power levers are pulled back) the fuel control unit sends less fuel to the engine to slow it down.

If there is an overspeed of the power turbine (N_2), the propeller governor will send a message to the fuel control unit, which will reduce fuel to the burner can to slow the power turbine.

Engine Start

Either 23 volts of battery power or the use of external power with at least 20 volts of battery power is needed to start an engine. The starter switches are located on the pilot's left subpanel. They are three position switches with the center being OFF, up ON, and down STARTER ONLY.

When the switch is placed up in the ON position, the starter/generator, standby fuel pump, and igniter plugs are energized. When held in the lower STARTER ONLY position, only the starter/generator is energized.

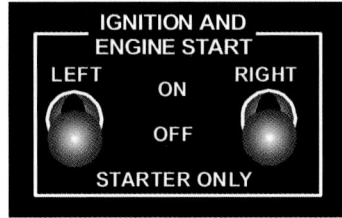

When ready to start, place the start switch to the UP position. The green [IGNITION ON] annunciator will illuminate, and the fuel pressure light will extinguish. When N_1 stabilizes above 12%, bring the condition lever out of cutoff to low idle. The ITT should begin to rise within 10 seconds (usually rises in about 2 seconds). Monitor the N_1 and ITT gauge (ITT should not exceed the dashed red line 1000° C). Check oil pressure and when the engine stabilizes at idle speed (above 50% N_1), turn the start switch OFF and hold the generator switch to reset for approximately one second to turn the starter into a generator. Bring the condition lever to high idle to help recharge the battery faster.

If ignition occurs within 20 seconds of any start attempt, there is no limit on the amount of time the starter can be on for that start. If a normal start occurs but you need to shut down the engine and restart it there is a 3 minute cool down time for the start starting when the starter was turned off.

If the [IGNITION ON] annunciator does not illuminate within 10 seconds of turning the start switch on, turn the starter off. If the engine doesn't start (no rise in ITT) within 10 seconds of brining the condition lever out of cutoff, move the condition lever to cutoff and hold the start switch to starter only for 10 seconds. This purges the engine of any residual fuel and helps it to cool. If the starter is used to motor the engine without the intention to start it there is a limitation on the starter of 20 seconds on, 5 minutes off.

If ignition (rise in ITT) occurs within 20 seconds of any start attempt, there is no limit on the time the starter can be engaged for that start.

Hung Start

A hung start can occur when there is a problem with the fuel nozzles. If the primary fuel nozzles kick in but are not working properly, there can be a non-centered flame which will cause a rapidly rising ITT. Another situation that may cause this is if the secondary fuel nozzles do not kick in. In these first two cases, ITT will rise rapidly and the engine will rotate at a low N_1 (40-45%). A third situation that can cause a hung start is if no fuel gets introduced. The indication of this happening is N_1 will stabilize around 15% (the maximum starter speed). In any of these cases, bring the condition lever to cutoff before the ITT reaches 1000° C or after 10 seconds, whichever comes first, then hold the start switch to STARTER ONLY for 10 seconds. Do not try another start. Consult maintenance.

Hot Start

A hot start occurs when there is a rapidly rising ITT. This could be caused by a weak battery when starting with the battery only. If this happens, bring the condition lever to cutoff before the ITT reaches 1000° C and hold the start switch to STARTER ONLY for 10 seconds and consult maintenance.

Auto Ignition

In addition to engine start, the engine ignitors can be used to help prevent an engine flame out caused by icing, precipitation, or turbulence. The auto ignition system will turn on the ignitors when engine torque falls below approximately 700 foot pounds. A green [L or R IGNITION ON] annunciator will illuminate when the igniters have been armed and are receiving power.

The 1900 is the only version of the King Air where auto ignition does not need to be turned on for landing. The reason for this is the PT6A-67D engine has four stages of axial compression while the other King Air's engines only have three. This extra stage of compression ensures there will be enough airflow at low power settings so the engine will not flame out when the power is at idle.

Notes:

Chapter 3
ANNUNCIATORS

Virtually all major systems and components in the airplane are monitored, and if a failure is sensed, it will illuminate an annunciator light in the cockpit to advise the pilot of a fault or a reminder that a certain condition exists. There are three types of annunciators; warning, caution, and advisory. Warning annunciator lights are red and are clustered together in the center of the glareshield. Caution lights are yellow, advisory lights either green or white, and both types are clustered together in the center of the lower panel just above the pedestal.

There is an illustration of the annunciator display panels in the back of this chapter. The reason for the illumination of each annunciator is noted below each illustration. The memory or checklist item associated with each annunciator can be found in the airplane flight manual.

Warning Annunciator

A warning annunciator requires immediate action by memory by the pilot. For example, low engine oil pressure will set off a warning annunciator. When a warning annunciator illuminates, it sets off a flashing red light called a master warning flasher. There are two master warning flashers; one in front of the pilot and the other in front of the co-pilot on the glareshield. The purpose of the master flasher is to gain the pilot's attention. After the master warning flasher has gained your attention, look at the annunciator panel to see which annunciator set it off. After noting which annunciator is illuminated, you should cancel the master warning flasher by pressing the face of the light. There are two benefits to canceling the flasher. One is to stop it from distracting you from dealing with the problem. The second is to reset it so if another warning annunciator illuminates, it will regain your attention that another problem exists. Pressing the master warning flasher will not do anything to the warning annunciator that illuminated. That will remain illuminated until the problem is corrected.

If you note on the warning annunciator display in the back of the chapter there are twenty five red warning annunciators and only seventeen with wording on them. One of the reasons for this is so the bulbs behind the annunciators without wording can be used as temporary replacements if a bulb behind an annunciator with wording were to burn out. Each warning annunciator is illuminated by two bulbs for additional protection against annunciators not illuminating when a fault is sensed.

Caution Annunciator

A caution annunciator requires consulting with a checklist to deal with the problem. A caution annunciator covers a component that is not quite as critical as a warning annunciator. For example, a generator failing will cause a caution annunciator to illuminate. When a caution annunciator illuminates, it sets off a yellow master caution flasher. The master caution flashers are located next to the master warning flashers on the glareshield. The same principal applies from the warning annunciator in dealing with the master caution flasher. After noting which caution annunciator is illuminated, cancel the master caution flasher by pressing the face of the light. The caution and advisory annunciator panel is located in the center of the lower portion of the instrument panel.

Advisory Annunciator

The advisory annunciator lights indicate that a system is operating under certain conditions. They tell you if something is on or off. For example, when fuel is transferring, an advisory annunciator illuminates to remind you of the situation. There are no checklist procedures to complete with advisory items since they are just advising the pilot of a condition. There are no flashers associated with advisory items to gain the pilots attention. There is no significance between the white or green advisory annunciators other than they are different colors.

Annunciator Power Source

Underneath the cabin floor is a series of printed circuit boards (PCB) that contain all the circuitry that illuminates each annunciator. Should there be a failure in one or all of the PCBs a yellow [ANN PWR SOURCE] annunciator will illuminate. This will alert you that some or all of the annunciators are not functioning.

Optional Annunciators

Certain annunciators are only added if the optional accessory equipment associated with that annunciator is installed in the aircraft. For example, the red warning [LAVATORY SMOKE] annunciator is added only in aircraft that have a lavatory installed.

The following 4 warning annunciators are only installed if the associated equipment is installed:

- Lavatory Smoke
- A/P Trim Fail
- A/P Fail
- Arm Emer Lites

The following 8 caution annunciators are only installed if the associated equipment is installed:

- Prop Gnd Sol
- L and R Bk Di Ovht
- Anti Skid Fail
- Pwr Steer Fail
- Man Steer Fail
- Pitch Trim Off
- Yd/Rb Fail (on aircaft without an autopilot)

The following 4 advisory annunciators are only installed if the associated equipment is installed:

- Pwr Steer Enga
- L and R Bk Deice On
- Rdr Pwr On

Testing and Dimming

To test the annunciator lights, a press-to-test switch is located to the right of the warning annunciators on the glareshield. When the switch is pressed, all of the annunciators will illuminate.

The annunciator display can be dimmed for nighttime operation. There are five things that need to occur for the annunciators to automatically dim.

- a generator is online
- overhead flood light is off
- pilot's flight instrument lights are on
- ambient light sensor (located on overhead panel) senses light below a preset value
- master light switch is on

There are two types of annunciators that will not dim at night due to their importance in getting the attention of the pilots. One type is the master warning flashers and the other is the engine fire annunciators.

Fire Detection System

A fire detection system monitors the engine compartment for excessive heat that would indicate an engine fire. A fire cable that forms a continuous loop around the engine is connected to a control amplifier that controls the fire detection system.

Electrical power is supplied to the fire detection system from the center bus. For the fire detection system to detect a fire and annunciate it in the cockpit the center bus must be receiving power from the battery or a generator.

Fire Cable and Control Amplifier

The fire cable is made up of a center conductor enclosed by a dielectric (temperature sensitive) circuit surrounded by a stainless steal outer coating for protection. The cable measures average resistance in Ohms along its entire length. As temperature increases, resistance decreases. The control amplifier reads the resistance value of the cable, compensates for outside air temperature, and illuminates the fire annunciator when resistance drops below a preset value.

If the continuous cable loop breaks, it still decreases in resistance with an increase in temperature, allowing the control amplifier to sense a fire. Because the length of the cable will decrease with a break, it will take hotter temperatures to decrease the resistance for the control amplifier to detect a fire. The control amplifier has a time delay set into it to prevent false fire warnings due to a short in the system.

The fire loop is continuously monitored. If a fault occurs, a yellow [L or R FIRE LOOP] annunciator illuminates, indicating that the fire detector circuit may not function properly.

Fire Detection Annunciator

When the control amplifier senses a fire, the respective L or R firewall fuel valves illuminate with red lights and the master warning annunciators will flash. The

| FIRE PULL |

firewall fuel valves, labeled FIRE PULL, are clear T-shaped handles located in the center of the instrument panel. Pulling this handle does two things, shuts off fuel to the engine and arms the fire bottle.

The fire extinguisher switch is the control for the extinguishing system. The switches are located on either side of the warning annunciator display on the glareshield. The annunciator switch is guarded by a clear plastic overlay to prevent inadvertent bumping of the switch. The wording on the switch was changed in aircraft serial number 93. The switch has three different annunciator sections; the upper half, lower right, and lower left. The upper half, placarded either L or R ENG FIRE PUSH TO EXT (UE 1 to UE 92 and is red) or EXTINGUISHER PUSH (UE 93 and after and is yellow), illuminates once the T-handle has been pulled indicating the fire bottle is armed. The lower right section of the annunciator, placarded OK, is green and is used when testing the system. The lower left, placarded D (UE 1 to UE 92) DISH (UE 93 and after), is yellow and illuminates anytime the extinguishing agent has been discharged.

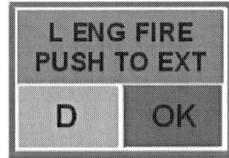

UE-1 to UE-92

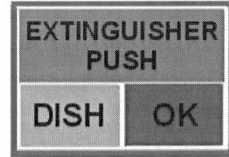

UE-93 and after

Fire Extinguishing

A fire bottle containing 2.1 pounds of Halon pressurized to between 320 and 370 psi (at 70° F) is located in each main gear wheel well. As a general rule the gauge should indicate between 200 and 500 psi.

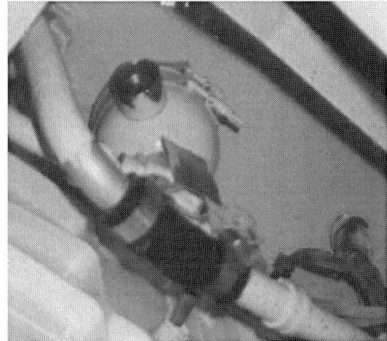

There is an explosive squib (like a 22 caliber bullet) that puts a hole in the base of the fire bottle to release the Halon. Once released, Halon is distributed through two tubes to the exhaust and accessory sections of the engine. Once activated, the entire supply of Halon is released. There is a gauge on each fire bottle to check the charge level prior to flight. Once discharged, the D or DISCH light illuminates indicating the bottle is now empty or discharged.

Fire Detection and Extinguisher Test

On the copilots side lower panel are the switches to test the fire extinguishing and detection system. There are four separate switches to test the extinguishing and detection system on both the left and right engines.

The extinguishing test switches are spring loaded to the middle off position with two test positions, up for test A and down for test B. The two test positions test the dual circuitry leading to the explosive squib in the fire bottles. When selecting test A, the yellow D or DISC and green OK light should illuminate on the fire detection annunciator. When selecting test B, only the green OK light should illuminate.

The fire detection test is also a three position switch spring loaded to the center "OFF" position. When holding the right or left switch up to the LOOP position, the appropriate L or R FIRE LOOP caution annunciator and master caution flasher should illuminate. This indicates the fire cable that loops around the engine is in good condition. When either switch is held down to the AMP position, the red light in the "Fire Pull" T-handle should illuminate. This indicates the circuitry in the control amplifier is working properly.

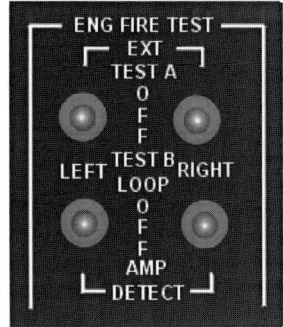

Warning Annunciator Display

L FUEL PRES LO	CABIN ALT HI	LAVATORY SMOKE	CABIN DIFF HI	R FUEL PRES LO
L OIL PRES LO	L ENVIR FAIL	CABIN DOOR	R ENVIR FAIL	R OIL PRES LO
————	L AC BUS	CARGO DOOR	R AC BUS	————
L BL AIR FAIL	A/P TRIM FAIL	ARM EMER LITES	A/P FAIL	R BL AIR FAIL
————	————	————	————	————

L or R FUEL PRES LO ... Fuel pressure less than 10 psi.

L or R OIL PRES .... Oil pressure below 60 psi.

L or R BL AIR FAIL .... EVA tubing has detected a rupture in the bleed air line or system is off.

CAB ALT HI .... Cabin altitude exceeds 10,000 feet.

L or R ENVIR FAIL .... Bleed air overtemp (500° F) or overpressure (44 psi) in environmental system.

L or R AC BUS .... AC bus has inoperative inverter.

A/P TRIM FAIL .... Out of trim or no trim command with autopilot on.

LAVATORY SMOKE .... Smoke in lavatory (if lavatory installed).

CABIN DOOR .... Cabin entry door is open or not locked.

CARGO DOOR .... Cargo door is open or not locked.

ARM EMER LITES .... Emergency light controls disarmed.

CABIN DIFF HI .... Cabin pressure differential exceeds 5.25 psi.

A/P FAIL .... A failure has occurred in the autopilot computer.

Caution/Advisory Annunciator Display

L DC GEN	L FUEL QTY	STALL HEAT	BATTERYCHARGE	PROP GND SOL	R FUEL QTY	R DC GEN
L FW VALVE	L COL TANK LOW	L GEN TIE OPEN	BATT TIE OPEN	R GEN TIE OPEN	R COL TANK LOW	R FW VALVE
L ENG ICE FAIL	L BK DI OVHT	HYD FLUID LOW	ANTI SKID FAIL	ANNPWRSOURCE	R BK DI OVHT	R ENG ICE FAIL
L FIRE LOOP	L PITOT HEAT	XFR VALVE FAIL	PWR STEER FAIL	MAN STEER FAIL	R PITOT HEAT	R FIRE LOOP
L NO AUX XFR	AUTOFTHER OFF	————	PITCH TRIM OFF	————	AFX DISABLE	R NO AUX XFR
INBD WG DEICE	YD/RB FAIL	————	TAIL DEICE	————	RUD BOOST OFF	OUTBD WG DEICE
L AUTOFEATHER	L IGNITION ON	————	PWRSTEERENGA	————	R IGNITION ON	R AUTOFEATHER
L ENG ANTI-ICE	L BK DEICE ON	————	MAN TIES CLOSE	————	R BK DEICE ON	R ENG ANTI-ICE
L ENVIR OFF	RDR PWR ON	FUEL TRANSFER	TAXI LIGHT	————	EXTERNALPOWER	R ENVIR OFF

Yellow Caution Annuncitors

L or R DC GEN .... Generator is off line.

L or R FW VALVE .... Fuel valve has not reached selected position.

L or R ENG ICE FAIL .... Ice vane has not reached selected position.

L or R FIRE LOOP .... Engine fire detection sense loop is open.

L or R NO AUX XFR ...... No fuel transfer from auxiliary to main tank.

L or R FUEL QTY .... Less than 324 pounds of usable fuel remaining.

L or R COL TANK LOW Less than 53 pounds of usable fuel remaining.

L or R BK DI OVHT .... EVA tubing has sensed bleed air leak in brake de-ice line.

L or R PITOT HEAT .... Pitot tube not receiving enough power to prevent icing or is not turned on.

AUTOFEATHER OFF .... Autofeather system is off and landing gear is extended.

YD RB FAIL .... A failure has occurred in the selected YD/RB computer (aircraft without an autopilot)

STALL HEAT .... Stall warning system not receiving enough power to prevent icing.

L or R GEN TIE OPEN ... Generator bus is isolated from center bus.

HYD FLUID LOW .... Landing gear hydraulic fluid level is low.

XFR VALVE FAIL .... Fuel transfer valve in transit for more than 2 seconds.

BATTERY CHARGE...... Excessive charge rate on battery.

BAT TIE OPEN............... Battery is isolated from generator bus.

ANTI SKID FAIL............ Hydraulic pressure low or electrical failure in anti skid system.

PWR STEER FAIL.......... Hydraulic pressure low or electrical failure in power steering system.

PITCH TRIM OFF........... Pitch trim was selected off with the switch on the yoke and switch on the pedestal is still on.

ANN PWR SOURCE ...... Power loss to some annunciator lights.

MAN STEER FAIL......... Power steering did not disconnect with the switch off. Nose gear will not free caster with power steering not engaged.

AFX DISABLE................ System has disarmed autofeather on side opposite of engine failure.

RUD BOOST OFF........... Rudder boost system is turned off.

PROP GND SOL .... Failure in the low pitch stop solenoid system.

Green Advisory Annunciators

INBD WG DEICE .... Air pressure in inboard wing de-ice boots is adequate.

L or R AUTOFEATHER . Autofeather is armed.

L or R ENG ANTI-ICE ... Ice vane is extended.

L or R IGNITION ON ..... Ignitors are selected on and powered.

L or R BK DEICE ON..... Brake de-ice is energized.

TAIL DEICE................... Air pressure in tail de-ice boots is adequate.

PWR STEER ENGA .... Power steering operational.

MAN TIES CLOSE......... Generator bus ties have been manually closed.

OUTBD WG DEICE .... Air pressure in outboard wing de-ice boots is adequate.

White Advisory Annunciators

L or R ENVIR OFF .... Bleed air valve is in the environmental off position.

RDR PWR ON................. Radar is on during ground operations.

FUEL TRANSFER.......... Fuel transfer valve is open.

TAXI LIGHT.................. Taxi light is on and landing gear is retracted.

EXTERNAL POWER ..... External power is connected to aircraft.

Chapter 4
FLIGHT CONTROLS

There are two types of flight controls, primary and secondary. The primary flight controls consist of the ailerons, elevator, and rudder. Secondary flight controls are trim tabs, flaps, and a yaw damp system.

Primary Flight Controls

The primary flight controls, moved by push-pull rods, conventional cable systems, and bell cranks, are used to control the aircraft along the longitudinal, lateral, and vertical axis.

Ailerons and Elevator

The ailerons and elevator are controlled by the pilot's and copilot's yoke in the cockpit. The yokes are interconnected by a T-bar and chain assembly located behind the instrument panel. The ailerons are moved by cables routed through pulleys and bell cranks to adjustable push-pull rods attached to the ailerons. The elevator is also moved by cables routed through pulleys and bell cranks, but is connected by a torque tube.

Rudder

The rudder pedals are connected to the nose wheel by a direct linkage. The pedals are also connected to the rudder assembly in the tail by a bell crank and cables. As the gear is retracted, the nose gear straightener roller automatically straightens the wheel and disconnects the nose wheel steering link from the rudder pedals. The nose wheel can be turned 14° left or 12° right of center, using the rudder pedals. Sharper turns, up to 48° left or right of center, require brake pressure and differential power. The minimum wing tip turning radius using partial braking action and differential power is 41 feet 2 inches. This causes excessive wear on the tires and should be used sparingly.

To enhance handling characteristics, the rudder and ailerons are interconnected. This means when you turn the control wheel (moving the ailerons) the rudder will also move to aid in coordination.

Secondary Flight Controls

Secondary flight controls are used to assist the primary flight controls to move the aircraft along the longitudinal, lateral, and vertical axis. They also may be used to control the aircraft if a primary flight control were to become jammed.

Trim Tabs

Movable trim tabs are located on the elevator, rudder and left aileron. The elevator trim can be controlled electrically, and all of the trim tabs can be manually controlled. The trim tabs are all moved by two push-pull rod attached to a jack screw and drum assembly for redundancy.

The electric pitch trim is controlled by thumb switches on the pilot's and copilot's yoke. The pilot's thumb switch will override the copilot's. An on/off switch for the electric trim is located on the pedestal and labeled ELEV TRIM. There is also a trim disconnect switch located on the yoke. It is a red, two-level push button type switch. The first level is used to disconnect the yaw damper, autopilot, and interrupts the rudder boost. When pressed to the second level, the electric elevator trim is disconnected. If the trim disconnect switch has been pressed and the on/off switch on the pedestal is on ("ELEV TRIM")
the [PITCH TRIM OFF] annunciator will illuminate. To reset the electric trim, cycle the switch "OFF" then to "ELEV TRIM."

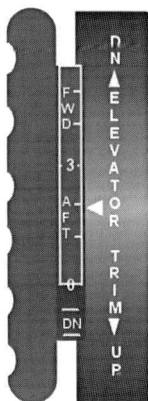

Prior to landing, the yaw damp system must be turned off. This is usually done with the red switch on the yoke (first level turns off yaw damp and autopilot). Because it is a two-level switch (like an auto focus camera) it is easy to press the switch all the way and accidentally disconnect the electric pitch trim.

The 1900 is usually landed with almost full aft trim, so if this happens and you don't notice the [PITCH

TRIM OFF] annunciator, the aircraft will not be trimmed properly for landing.

As a backup to the electric trim, there is a manual pitch trim wheel located just to the left of the power levers. It also serves as the indicator to where the pitch trim is at. Most captains learn to keep their leg lightly resting on the wheel to serve as the first indication of a runaway electric trim.

Flaps

There are two flaps installed on each wing; one on the center section, and one on the outer wing panel. The flaps are of fowler design, and individual jackscrew

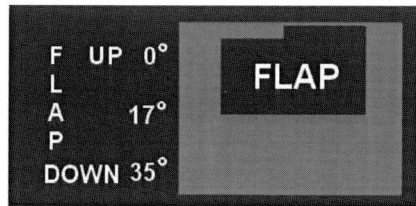

assemblies located on each flap are electrically powered from the left generator bus. The flap motor incorporates a magnetic clutch and potentiometer driven by the right inboard flap. The flap position indicator is operated by the potentiometer. There are three pre-select positions; up (0°), approach (17°), and down (35°). Limit switches located on the right inboard flap track will stop flap movement at these settings when selected.

The flaps cannot be stopped at an intermediate position.

The airspeed limit for extension of the flaps to 17° is 188 KIAS. For extension of flaps beyond 17° airspeed must be less than 143 KIAS for aircraft with serial numbers UE 1 to 78 and less than 154 KIAS for aircraft with serial numbers UE 79 and after.

When the flaps are selected beyond 17° with the landing gear not down and locked, the landing gear warning horn will sound continuously. Unlike when the warning horn sounds when power levers are retarded, you are not able to cancel the horn (unless the landing gear is down and locked) when the flaps are extended beyond 17°.

A safety mechanism stops power to the flap motor and stops flap movement when a flap is 3° to 6° out of sync with the other flap on the same side.

Lowering the flaps in flight results in a nose up pitching moment that requires retrimming of the aircraft. Additional effects include reduced airspeed for a specific power setting and a reduced stalling speed.

Yaw Damp

The yaw damp system keeps the tail from swinging side to side and aids the pilot with directional control. A yaw sensor incorporated in the compass system senses changes in heading and transmits a signal (115 volt AC) to a yaw control valve. When the system senses the need, the corresponding rudder boost solenoid is opened, allowing regulated bleed air at 10 psi to reposition the appropriate rudder servo providing yaw dampening. The system should be off for take-off and landing. The yaw damp is normally turned on above 400 feet AGL and turned off prior to landing. A "YD" annunciator on the EADI illuminates when the system is on.

Rudder Boost

The rudder boost is used to help a pilot maintain coordination during an engine failure. The rudder boost computer monitors the torque on both engines. When approximately a 1200 foot pound split occurs between the two engines, rudder boost servos will apply rudder pressure to the operative engine side. The greater the torque differential, the more the rudder deflection. The rudder boost can be de-activated by a switch on the center pedestal or by depressing and holding the pilot or copilot yoke switch to the first level. When the rudder boost is turned off a yellow [RUD BOOST OFF] annunciator will illuminate.

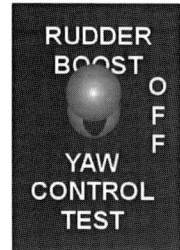

The yaw control test checks the circuitry of the rudder boost and yaw damp annunciator lights. When the switch is held to the "YAW CONTROL TEST" position the yellow [RUD BOOST OFF] and [YD RB FAIL] annunciators should illuminate.

Autopilot

The autopilot can control the aircraft along the vertical, lateral, and longitudinal axis. To engage the autopilot push the A/P ENG button on the pedestal.

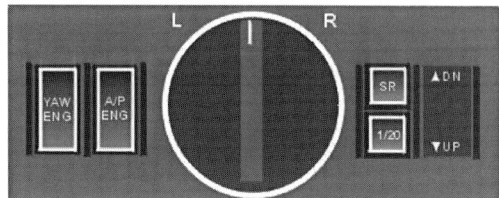

The mode control panel on the cockpit panel controls the autopilot. It can be set to follow the heading bug, track a course in the nav mode, follow a localizer and glide slope in the approach mode, or track a localizer with reverse sensing on a back course. It will also climb or descend at a selected vertical speed, indicated airspeed, or via a selected pitch.

There are two warning annunciators associated with the autopilot. The [A/P FAIL] annunciator alerts you to a failure in the autopilot computer. The [A/P TRIM FAIL] annunciator alerts you that the autopilot is not supplying a trim command to the aircraft or the aircraft is out of trim. Once the aircraft reaches a limit of out of trim with the autopilot on, the autopilot will automatically turn off in an out of trim condition.

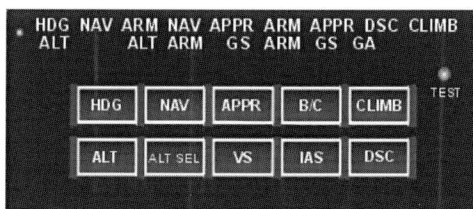

Notes:

Chapter 5
PROPELLERS

The propellers on the 1900 are four-bladed, composite, constant-speed, full-feathering, fully reversible propellers. The composite propeller is made up of a honeycomb mesh with titanium leading edges. The thin titanium outer shell prevents blade erosion from rock chips. Only the paint will chip away. The propeller will maintain a constant diameter of 110 inches. This leaves a ground clearance of 13.5 inches below the propeller.

The propeller maintains a constant speed through the use of a primary propeller governor. There are two backup governors, one of which is also used to govern propeller rpm while on the ground. Like most constant speed propellers, rpm is maintained with oil pressure being routed to and from the propeller hub moving a piston to adjust the pitch of the propeller. The only additional component this propeller governor has over one you would find in a piston airplane is a movable low pitch stop, which allows it to have negative blade angles to help slow the aircraft on the ground.

Propeller Blade Angle

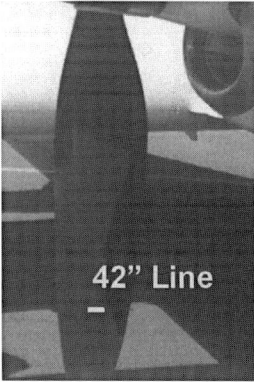

42" Line

The blade angle is measured 42 inches from the propeller hub. This is referred to as the 42 inch station and is denoted on the propeller by a thin yellow line. Blade angles vary from 79° in the feathered position to -14.5° in maximum reverse. The reason the blade does not go to 90° in feather is because this would cause the blade to produce lift and cause induced drag, which would take away from the single engine performance of the aircraft. With the blade only going to 79°, it does create slightly more parasite drag due to an increase in exposed surface area, but not as much as the induced drag would cause if the blade went to 90°. The cruise blade angle is normally between 30° and 45°. There are four low pitch stops; flight idle at 12.7°, ground idle at 4.9°, ground fine at –5.9°, and maximum reverse at –14.5°.

Propeller Governors

There are three propeller governors; primary, fuel topping, and overspeed. They are sequential in operation, meaning that only one is working to maintain propeller rpm at a time, and if the primary fails there is one to back it up. If the backup fails, there is a backup to that one also. The primary governor will maintain propeller speed from 1200 to 1700 rpm. The fuel topping governor maintains propeller rpm on the ground at 96% what you have selected with the propeller lever in the cockpit; and in the air, in the event of a primary governor failure, to 106% of selected propeller rpm. The overspeed governor is set to maintain the rpm in the event of a primary governor failure to 1802 rpm (106% of maximum). A schematic of the propeller governor system is located in the back of this chapter. For a detailed discussion of how a propeller governor works see Appendix A.

Primary Governor

The primary governor is located on top of the engine near the propeller hub and controls propeller rpm in the normal governor range (1400-1700 rpm). For all normal air operations, it maintains prop rpm to what you have selected in the cockpit. Typical cruise prop setting is 1550 rpm. The propeller governor maintains an oil pressure of 750 psi to create instantaneous blade angle changes.

The only difference between a basic propeller governor and the primary propeller governor is a movable low pitch stop. A propeller governor with a fixed low pitch stop will act the same as one with a movable low pitch stop while in the air. For example, when coming in to land and the airspeed decreases to the final approach speed, propeller rpm will began to decrease below what you have selected. This is not because you are not producing enough oil pressure to maintain propeller rpm, it is because you are at the low pitch stop. If there were no low pitch stop, the propeller blade angle would continue to decrease to negative values as the primary governor continues to send oil into the hub in an attempt to maintain rpm. This would cause airflow in the opposite direction through the propellers, dramatically decreasing aircraft performance. When the propellers reach the low pitch stop, the blade angle becomes fixed, and the primary governor will no longer be able to maintain the selected rpm. You can tell when the propellers are on the low pitch stop because the propeller rpm drops below what you have selected in the cockpit.

Movable low pitch stop

On a basic propeller governor, the low pitch stop is built into the propeller construction. In the 1900, it needs to be movable so you can select negative blade angles on the ground to help slow the airplane. This is done through a beta valve (see diagram in back of chapter). The beta valve will cut off oil pressure to the primary governor, so no matter how far the pilot valve lowers (opening the valve for oil to go to the propeller) there will be no oil available.

The propeller hub moves along a set of four rails as the blade angle changes. When the blade angle reaches approximately 18°, it reaches the point on the rails where it begins to move the reverse lever that is connected to the beta valve. When the blade angle reaches 12.7°, the beta valve has moved to completely cut off oil to the primary governor. On the diagram, note where the reverse lever is pivoted. As the collar moves to the right along the slip ring, the beta valve also moves to the right, cutting off oil to the primary governor.

There are three times the beta valve gets repositioned so oil pressure is allowed to go back to the primary governor. This, in a sense, resets the low pitch stop. One time is when the aircraft lands and the right main squat switch activates an electrical solenoid, moving the beta valve to allow the propeller blade angle to move to 4.9°. The other two times are when the power levers are moved over the detents into ground fine and reverse. This resets the location of the low pitch stop by moving the rails that the propeller hub moves on so that new blade angles will make the beta valve move.

There are micro switches in the power levers that will override the squat switch to move the blade angle from 12.7° to 4.9°. Be careful not to lift up on the power levers in flight when they are at idle, or the blade angle will decrease and cause a loss in performance.

The [PROP GND SOL] annunciator illuminates when a failure occurs in the low pitch stop solenoid system. If the annunciator illuminates on the ground it indicates one side or both low pitch stop solenoids are not being powered and in the flight mode. If the annunciator illuminates in flight it indicates one side or both solenoids are being powered and in the ground mode. If the failure occurs in flight, the propeller will move below the flight idle pitch of 12.7° to 4.9° when the aircraft slows on approach. If only one propeller low pitch solenoid is affected this will cause the aircraft to yaw towards the lower pitch propeller. If both propellers are affected there will be a decreasing performance affect on the aircraft. Power can be removed from the solenoid by pulling the 10 amp PROP GND circuit breaker. Refer to the abnormal procedures section of the AFM for a modified approach procedure if the [PROP GND SOL] annunciator illuminates in flight.

NOTE: The propeller will maintain selected rpm even after an engine failure. The windmilling engine circulates enough oil to continue to run the primary governor. Therefore, you must feather the propeller after an engine failure to avoid this condition.

Overspeed Governor

The overspeed governor protects the propeller system in the event of a primary governor failure. How it works is identical to the primary governor, with the exception that the speeder spring is not connected to the propeller levers. It has a predetermined tension, so the only time it will raise the pilot valve is when the propeller reaches 106% of maximum, or 1802 rpm. This will dump oil pressure and increase the blade angle to maintain the 1802 rpm.

Fuel Topping Governor

The fuel topping governor also protects the propeller system in the event of a primary governor failure. In addition, it governs the propeller system at 96% of selected while on the ground and is set to take over in the air at 106% of selected rpm. The rpm is controlled on the ground at 96% so that you will not get maximum rpm while the propeller blade angles are in reverse. As long as the propellers are set to anything below full rpm (1700), the fuel topping governor will take over before the overspeed governor to maintain rpm in the event of a primary governor failure. The fuel topping governor controls propeller rpm through the engine fuel control unit. If propeller speed exceeds the limits, fuel flow will be reduced to the engine to keep the propellers on speed.

If the propeller levers are not full forward and the primary governor fails in flight, it will look like there has been an engine failure. The fuel topping governor takes over and will significantly reduce the amount of fuel to the engine to maintain propeller rpm. If you have what looks like an engine failure, make sure to bring the propeller levers full forward to reset the fuel topping governor and restore the proper amount of fuel to the engine in case it was a primary governor failure. With the propeller levers full forward a primary governor failure can then be noted by rpm's stabilizing at 1802 rpm.

NOTE After touchdown, the non-flying pilot should bring the propeller levers full forward to assure maximum reverse thrust is available. You can do this on short final, but it makes noise that may disturb the passengers. It is advised that you bring the propeller levers full forward on short final to help slow the aircraft if you are making a no flap landing.

Propeller Governor Test

The preflight checklist calls for the propeller system to be tested before the first flight of the day during the run up. During the overspeed and low pitch tests, the propeller levers need to be full forward. To test the overspeed governor, hold the switch (shown at the right), located on the pilot's lower left subpanel, to the "OVERSPEED" position while increasing power. During the test, the overspeed governor is reset to approximately 1535 to 1595 rpm from its normal 1802 rpm. Propeller rpm should stabilize between 1535 and 1595 while the power levers are increased.

PROP TEST
OVERSPEED
O
F
F
LOW PITCH

To test the low pitch solenoid, set the power levers to achieve 1500 rpm on the propellers. Hold the prop test switch to "LOW PITCH" and both propeller rpm should drop approximately 250 rpm.

Another pre-takeoff test for the propeller system is to manually feather the propellers like you do in any piston aircraft with a constant speed propeller. You are just checking to make sure the propellers will feather. Although fresh oil circulates into the propeller hub each time you manually feather the propeller, that is not a reason for the check because a transfer gland in this system constantly cycles fresh warm oil into the propeller hub.

Power Levers

The power lever settings are broken down into three sections; the alpha, beta, and reverse range. The alpha range adjusts the fuel flow to the engine through the fuel control unit to set the engine speed you have selected. The alpha range is selected by the power levers from the idle stop to full forward.

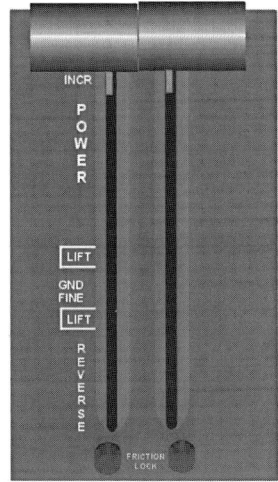

In the beta range, the power levers control the beta valve to reduce propeller blade angle without having an effect on gas generator speed. The beta range is selected by lifting up on the power levers when they are at the alpha range idle stop and moving them aft.

In the reverse range, the power levers adjust the blade angle of the propeller, engine speed for reverse power, and reset the fuel topping governor from its airborne 106% to the ground setting of 96%. The reverse range is selected by lifting up and moving the power levers aft when they are at the back stop of the beta range.

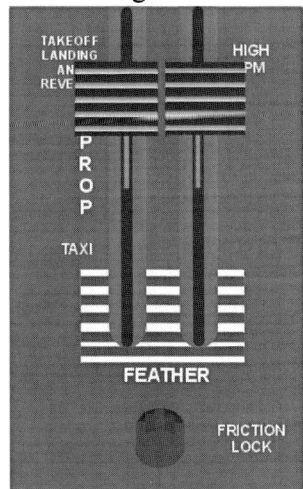

Propeller Levers

The propeller control levers in the cockpit adjust the propeller rpm from 1200 to 1700. There is a taxi detent for the propeller levers at the low rpm end that will keep the propeller rpm in the ground taxi range of

950 to 1250 rpm. The taxi detent also prevents inadvertent movement of the propeller into feather. When the propeller levers are moved past this detent into feather, the pilot valve in the governor is held in the full up position allowing all the oil to flow from the hub to the engine oil sump. Since the propeller shaft and the gas generator shaft are not connected, the propeller can be feathered while the engine is running. This should only be done when the engine is at idle to prevent excessive loads on the propeller gearbox.

N_2 Gauge

The N_2 gauge displays propeller rpm. There are two red arcs that are only limitations for ground operations. Propeller rpm's between 400-950 and 1250-1395 are prohibited on the ground. The red line at 1700 shows the maximum propeller rpm for ground or flight operations.

Autofeather

The propeller system is equipped with an autofeathering control. This is used to automatically feather the propeller in the event of an engine failure. The benefits of the system, versus the pilot having to manually feather it, is for speed of feathering and determination of which engine failed. The system should be armed during takeoff, climb, descent, and landing. The switch to arm the system is located on the pilot's lower left subpanel. The switch alone will not arm the system. To arm the system, the switch must be set to "ARM", and both power levers need to be advanced to a position that equals above approximately 90% N_1 which will cause the torque to increase above the high pressure torque sensor of 1000 foot pounds to arm the system. There is a micro switch in the power lever quadrant which must be passed and due to rigging, may require a slightly different power setting. When the system is armed, four green annunciators illuminate and one yellow annunciator extinguishes. Two green [L and R AUTOFEATHER] annunciators are located on the caution/advisory panel, and two green [AFX] annunciators are located next to the torque gauges.

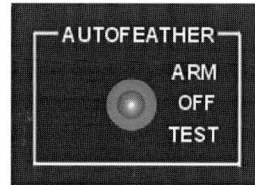

Should there be a loss of torque on an engine indicating failure, the system will first disarm the opposite autofeather when engine torque drops below 750 foot pounds. Once disarming the opposite autofeather, the yellow [AFX DISABLE] (autofeather disabled) annunciator will illuminate and the green [AUTOFEATHER] and [AFX] will extinguish. When torque drops below 350 foot pounds, the propeller will automatically feather. An autofeather solenoid opens and creates a path of least resistance for oil to flow to the engine oil sump. The counterweights and spring push the oil out of the dome as the propellers feather.

If the autofeather switch is off and the landing gear extended, a caution [AUTOFEATHER OFF] annunciator will illuminate reminding you to arm the autofeather if appropriate.

Autofeather Test

To test the system, both power levers should be at 1000 foot pounds of torque and the autofeather switch placed to "TEST." With the system in the test mode, the power levers do not need to be advanced above 90% N_1. Bring one of the power levers to idle, and as engine torque drops below 750 foot pounds, the opposite autofeather will disarm itself. When engine torque drops below 350 foot pounds, the propeller will begin to feather. When the propeller feathers and the engine is still operating at idle speed, engine torque increases due to increased propeller blade angle. There is a 320-350 foot pound torque limit for the autofeather test. As the engine torque increases during the feather process, it exceeds the 320-350 foot pound limit, and the propeller begins to come out of feather. As it comes out of feather, propeller blade angle reduces, causing reduced engine torque. When engine torque falls below 350 foot pounds, the autofeather system will again feather the propeller. This cycle continues as long as the autofeather switch is held to the "TEST" position.

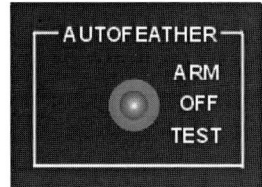

During the test, both autofeather annunciators should illuminate when the switch is placed in the "TEST" position. As power is reduced on one engine, the opposite annunciator should extinguish at approximately 525 foot pounds, and both annunciators should extinguish at approximately 320 foot pounds. During the test, the autofeather annunciator will cycle on and off with the fluctuations in torque. You should also hear the propeller cycle in and out of feather during the process. Also, if both power levers are reduced simultaneously, both annunciators should extinguish and neither propeller should feather.

During the autofeather test, the [AFX DISABLE] annunciator will illuminate, showing the pilot that the system has disengaged from the operating engine.

Propeller Synchrophaser and Synchroscope

There is a synchrophaser and synchroscope that work to match propeller rpm to reduce the wining noise that occurs when the propellers are out of sync.

The synchrophaser determines the speed of each propeller and matches the rpm of the slower propeller to the rpm of the faster one through the use of a control box connected to each primary governor. The switch to turn on the synchrophaser is located to the left of the oil pressure and temperature gauges. Because the synchrophaser operates in a limited range, you will need to manually move the propeller levers to get within the 10 rpm range to automatically sync them. To help you manually sync the propellers there is a synchroscope installed.

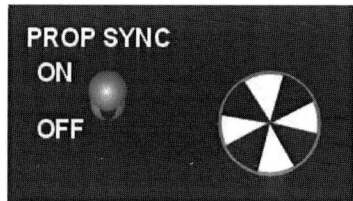

The synchroscope is a black and white cross-pattern dial that spins in the direction of the faster propeller. If the dial is spinning to the right, the right propeller lever is spinning faster than the left so either move the right propeller lever back or bring the left propeller lever forward.

Prop Governor
Beech 1900D

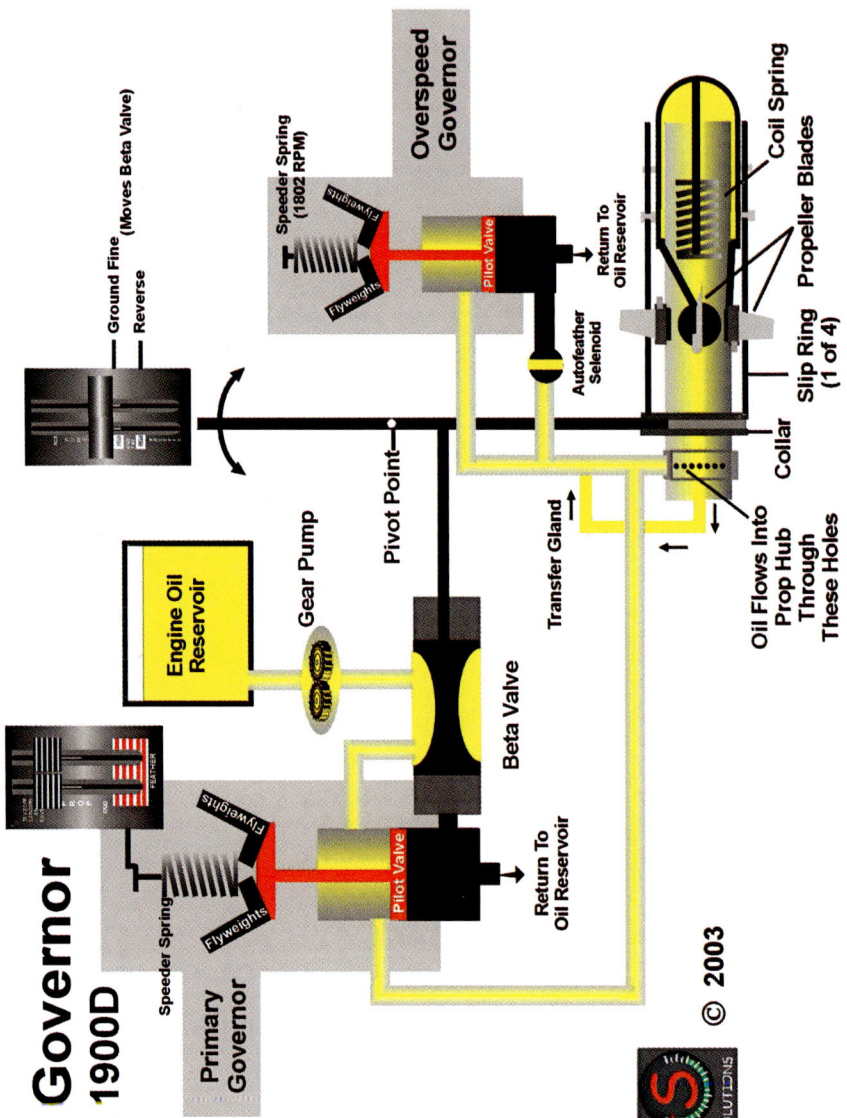

Primary Governor

Speeder Spring

Flyweights

Pilot Valve

Engine Oil Reservoir

Gear Pump

Pivot Point

Beta Valve

Return To Oil Reservoir

Ground Fine (Moves Beta Valve)

Reverse

Overspeed Governor

Speeder Spring (1802 RPM)

Flyweights

Pilot Valve

Return To Oil Reservoir

Autofeather Selenoid

Transfer Gland

Coil Spring

Propeller Blades

Slip Ring (1 of 4)

Collar

Oil Flows Into Prop Hub Through These Holes

© 2003

AVIATION SOLUTIONS

Chapter 6
ELECTRICAL SYSTEM

The electrical system is a 28.25 ± .25 volt direct current (DC) system. DC electrical power is provided by a 23 (36 optional) ampere-hour, 24 volt Nickel Cadmium (NiCad) battery, and two 300 ampere, 28 volt starter/generators. During normal operation, the starter/generators supply power to all DC buses and charge the battery. Alternating Current (AC) is supplied by two 400 Hz inverters supplying both 26 and 115 volts.

Definitions

Bus .... A distribution point for electricity. During normal operations buses are tied together for redundancy and to help dissipate heat. There are 6 buses in the electrical system; L and R generator bus, L and R Center bus, triple fed bus, and hot battery bus.

Schematic Symbol:

Left Generator Bus

Current Limiter ...... (Also known as a Slow Blow Fuse or a Jiffy Pop Fuse) A type of fuse used to isolate part of the system during a malfunction. When it senses a specific amount of heat it will blow (like a fuse would) not allowing current to flow through it. Unlike a fuse, though, it senses a specific amount of heat, not current, to make it blow.

Schematic Symbol:

250A

Diode...................... A one way valve that prevents electricity from flowing in both directions. It produces resistance in the line and uses one volt of electricity.

Schematic Symbol:

HED .... Hall Effect Device or High Energy Dissipater. They sense overexcitation (too many amps) in one direction and open a bus tie to isolate a part of the system during a malfunction. They can also sense a specific amount of voltage to limit when it will close. This saves battery power by preventing the generator buses from being connected to the battery before a generator comes on line.

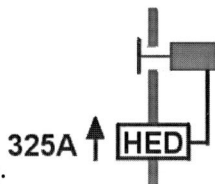

Schematic Symbol:

325A ↑ **HED**

Line Contactor .... A bridge in the electrical system that can control whether current flows through it or not. It takes electrical power to operate it. If electrical power is taken away it will fail to the open position. There are three types of line contactors; Relays, Switches and Ties.

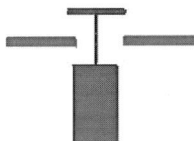

Schematic Symbol:

(Relay, Tie, and Basic Line Contactor)

Relay .... An automatic device that reacts to a current or voltage change by activating a switch in an electric circuit. It is a type of line contactor. In the airplane, we have unlimited control over opening or closing the circuit with a switch in the cockpit. (eg. START RELAY - start switch)

Tie .... The same as a relay but the aircraft electrical system has control over a tie to close and open it during normal operations. It is used to isolate part of the system during a malfunction.
(eg. GENERATOR BUS TIE)

Switch .... The same as a relay but we have limited control over a switch in the electrical system. It can open automatically (due to an overvoltage situation) or manually (with a switch in the cockpit), but it must be closed manually. (eg. GENERATOR SWITCH, BATTERY SWITCH)

Schematic Symbol:

NiCad..................... Nickel Cadium Battery. Used in most turbine
powered aircraft instead of a lead acid battery.

Schematic Symbol:

NiCad Battery

A 23 ampere-hour (optional 36 amp-hour), 24 volt, air cooled, NiCad
battery is located in the right wing root between the fuselage and the
right engine nacelle. The 23 ampere-hour means that a brand new, fully
charged battery can deliver one ampere of current for 23 hours without
being recharged. It also should be able to deliver 23 amperes for one
hour or any combination of amperes and hours that add up to 23. For
example, it can put out 11.5 amps for two hours. This rating system can
help determine how long the battery should last if both generators fail.

The battery switch is
located on the pilot's left
subpanel. When turned on,
battery power is connected
to the left and right center
bus and the triple fed bus.
This is done when the

	MASTER SWITCH	
ON		GEN RESET
OFF		
BATT	L GEN	R GEN

battery switch uses power from the battery to close the battery bus tie
and battery relay. See the electrical system diagram at the end of this
chapter.

The initial cost of a NiCad battery is several times higher than the cost of
a lead-acid battery. Even so, NiCad batteries are preferred over lead-acid
batteries for many reasons. In addition to low maintenance costs and
long service life, they also have a short recharge time, excellent
reliability, good starting capabilities, and are able to maintain a full
capacity of charge for a longer period of time before it discharges. One
disadvantage is that it develops a memory for the amount of charge
usually used and begins to think that amount of charge is its full capacity.
To compensate for that, the battery needs to be deep cycled. All of the
charge is taken out of the battery, which is then recharged slowly, to
prevent it from keeping this memory. Another disadvantage of a Nicad
battery is thermal runaway. This happens when there is damage to the
gas barrier between the different cells inside the battery due to
overcharging at a high rate under high temperatures. In a thermal

runaway the battery temperature continues to rise until the battery melts down and disintegrates.

Battery Charge Current Detector

When the battery is recharged from the aircraft electrical system at a rate above 6 amps in 6 seconds, an yellow [BATTERY CHARGE] light on the annunciator panel illuminates. This is considered a normal indication after a battery start of an engine. The annunciator should last no more than 5 minutes. If it does, turn the battery off and consult maintenance. Battery overheating also causes the [BATTERY CHARGE] light to illuminate due to increased battery charge current. If the annunciator illuminates in flight, the battery switch should be turned off to prevent a thermal runaway.

Battery Charge Current Check

Battery charge current is checked by turning one generator switch off. Selecting the battery switch off should not change the loadmeter reading by more than .025 (approximately 7 amps) and should cause the [BATTERY CHARGE] annunciator light to extinguish. A change greater than .025 indicates an overcharge. The battery charge current check should be done only on the ground.

Starter/Generator

The starter/generator is located on the accessory section of each engine. When the starter/generator is receiving power from the center bus, it turns into a starter for the engine. To turn it into a generator, the shaft to the accessory section of the engine must spool up beyond 52% N_1.

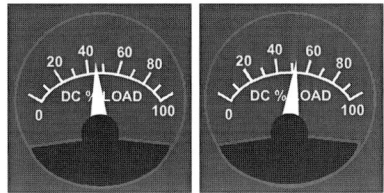

Each generator is capable of producing a continuous current of 300 amperes at 28 volts. Two volt/loadmeters, located on the overhead panel, indicate generator output.

The generator switches are two, three-position switches on the pilot's left subpanel. The switch can be placed in the lower "OFF" or middle "ON" position. The switch is spring loaded from the upper "GEN RESET" position to "ON." When held in the reset position for more than one

second, the generator turns on. Another time you would use the reset position is to turn the generator on if it is dropped off line due to an over voltage situation. Anytime a generator is not online a yellow [L or R DC GEN] annunciator will be illuminated.

Separate from the generator switches are two three-position starter switches located on the pilot's left subpanel. When placed in the "ON" position (up), the starter motors the gas generator shaft, turns the ignitors on, and energizes the standby electric boost pump. When held down in the "STARTER ONLY" position, the starter drives the gas generator shaft and leaves the ignitors and fuel pump off. When released, the switch returns to the center "OFF" position.

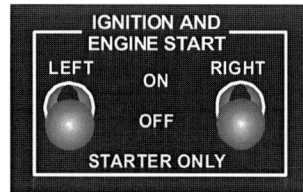

Initially, the starter draws 1100 amperes, which drops to about 300 amperes as turbine speed reaches 20%. During a cross generator start, the generator control unit will limit the operating generator to approximately 400 amps and de-energizes the 325 amp bus ties so the extra current is allowed to flow from the opposite generator through the center buses to the starter. The remaining 700 amps (1100 initially required for starter minus 400 which the generator produces) comes from the battery.

Operating time limits for the starter are:

- 20 seconds on, 30 seconds off
- 20 seconds on, 60 seconds off
- 20 seconds on, 5 minutes off

See the limitations section at the end of this chapter for details on the starter limits for different scenarios.

Two generator control units, the "brains" of the electrical system, are installed to provide the following:

- Voltage regulation (28.25 ± .25 volts) at all engine speeds, temperatures, and loads. During a cross start it will also energize extra coils to produce the additional current that a start requires.
- Line contactor control to connect the generator to the electrical buses. It also senses 28 volts to close the left and right generator bus ties.
- Over voltage and over excitation protection over 32 volts.
- Paralleling/load sharing within 10% when load exceeds 25%.

- Reverse current protection - if one generator falls below 28 volts it becomes a parasite to the system by drawing current from the other generator. If this happens the generator control unit will take the under excited (reverse current) generator off line by opening the line contactor.
- Cross start current limiting which de-energizes the HED during a start.

Generator Output Indication

There are three gauges used to see generator output. Two load meters measured in percentage of load and a voltmeter that monitors voltages on all buses by using the volt select switch.

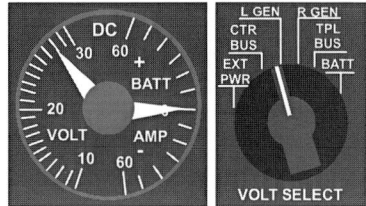

Electrical Distribution

The electrical distribution system is considered a triple-fed system, which indicates most buses are fed from three sources; battery and both generators. Distribution of electrical power is arranged so that components with complementary functions, such as the number 1 inverter and its control circuit, are on the same bus. Components with duplicate functions, such as left and right pitot heat, are on different buses. White rings around switches indicate that they are fed by either the center or triple-fed buses in addition to another bus for redundancy.

Buses

When the battery switch is turned on, power goes only to the center and triple-fed bus through a battery relay and bus tie. Power does not reach the generator buses because the battery only produces 24 volts and the generator bus ties will not close without 28 volts. This helps the battery to not deplete its energy so fast before you get a generator on line.

When the start switch is turned on, it closes the starter relay to connect the starter/generator to the center bus. As long as the center bus is receiving power from either the battery or external power, the starter/generator will begin to motor the gas generator shaft in the engine to initiate start sequence. After engine start, with the generator switch on, generator current is allowed to flow through the generator control unit and the volt/loadmeter to its respective generator bus. With the generator producing 28 volts and the battery producing only 24 volts, power from the generator buses is distributed throughout the system, and the battery is allowed to charge. The generator buses are connected to the center bus through 325 amp HEDs.

The triple fed bus receives power from three sources, both generator buses and the battery bus. To protect the electrical system in case of an electrical short on an item connected to the triple fed bus, there are 60 amp current limiters on each of the feeder lines. Should a current limiter sense over 60 amps through it, it will pop and not allow any more current to flow through it. There is no way to reset a current limiter from the cockpit. Once blown, maintenance must replace it. Each of the feeder lines to the triple fed bus also have a diode on it so power can not flow through the triple fed bus to any other bus.

Bus Tie

There are two types of bus ties; generator bus ties and a battery bus tie. One function of the generator bus ties was described above in not connecting the generator buses to the electrical system until a generator comes on line. In addition to isolating the generator buses from the rest of the electrical system when just the battery is on, the generator bus ties are also used to protect the system in case of a fault in one of the generator buses. If a short were to occur in the flap motor, (it is only powered by the left generator bus) it would try to draw all current toward the short. When over 325 amps in .010 seconds flows through the HED, it opens the left generator bus tie to isolate the short. A yellow [L or R GEN TIE OPEN] will illuminate once the generator bus tie opens.

The battery bus tie is used to help the generator bus ties isolate a short in the L or R center bus. A short on an item in the center bus will open both generator bus ties as described above but battery power can also feed a short in the center bus. In that situation the battery bus tie will sense over 275 amps in .012 seconds and open the battery bus tie isolating the center bus from the battery.

The bus tie system is controlled in the cockpit by two switches located on the pilot's lower left subpanel. To access a piece of equipment on the left or right generator bus with just the battery on, a GEN TIES switch can manually close the generator bus ties so power can reach the generator buses. During a dual generator failure, this switch can be used to access the flap motor. The switch should also be used to open the bus ties after the flaps are at their desired position so battery power is not depleted as

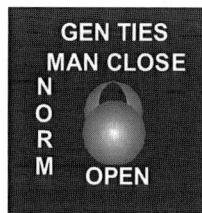

quickly. With the bus ties closed, a fully charged battery only lasts 8 to 10 minutes compared to 30 to 35 minutes when the bus ties are open. To alert you when the generator bus ties have been manually closed, quickly depleting battery power, a green [MAN TIES CLOSE] annunciator will illuminate.

The other switch used to control the bus tie system is the BUS SENSE switch. This switch is normally used during the run up before the first flight of the day. When the switch is placed to the test position, current is sent to all three of the HEDs, opening all of the bus ties. The [L and R GEN TIE OPEN] and [BATT TIE OPEN] annunciators illuminate indicating that all three bus ties are open. The switch also has a reset position. This function allows you to reset the HEDs in the event that a bus tie opened.

Hot Battery Bus

The components on the hot battery bus are powered regardless of the position of the battery switch. During normal operation, the hot battery bus is powered by the battery and both the left and right generators. The following items are connected to the hot battery bus:

- L and R engine fire extinguisher
- L and R firewall fuel shutoff valve
- External power annunciator and overvoltage sensor
- Door entry and aisle lights
- Cockpit emergency lights
- Control wheel clock
- Right pitot heater
- Ground com power
- Cargo compartment lights

NOTE: If these items are left on, even with the battery switch in the "OFF" position, battery power can be depleted.

External Power

An external power source may be connected to the aircraft electrical system to conserve battery power while starting the engines or when testing electrical equipment on the ground. The external power receptacle is located on the back side of the left engine nacelle. The power unit should be capable of delivering at least 1000 amperes during engine start, and a continuous load of 300 amperes at 28.0 to 28.4 volts.

Before connecting an external power unit, turn the battery on, and the generators, electrical systems, and avionics off to avoid damage due to electrical surges. When an external power source is connected to the aircraft, a white [EXTERNAL POWER] annunciator light will illuminate. Another time the annunciator may illuminate is in flight when moisture in the receptacle causes a false indication.

NOTE   The aircraft battery must indicate a charge of at least 20 volts before connecting external power.

AC Electrical System

Inverters

Inverters, located in the engine nacelles, convert DC power to AC power for aircraft systems. Although the items that use AC power can vary from airplane to airplane, here is a list of items that are normally powered by AC power in the 1900D:

- Radar
- Flight Data Recorder
- Attitude Indicators
- Nav 1 and 2
- RMI 1 and 2
- Engine Torque Meters
- Yaw Damp Sensor

The generator buses provide power to their respective inverters. If a generator bus fails, the center bus acts as a secondary source of power for the inverter. If one inverter fails, items normally powered from the inverter can

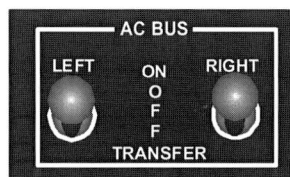

be powered by the opposite inverter by selecting transfer on the respective AC Bus switch.

The inverters are rated at 400Hz, and 115 volts for avionics components, 26 volts for engine instruments. Inverter failure warning is provided by a red [L or R AC BUS] annunciator to alert the pilot that the respective AC bus has an inoperative inverter.

If both generators fail, certain items that are AC powered automatically lose power. This is done by having these items connected to an AC shed bus. When a dual generator failure happens, all the items on the AC shed bus lose power. Also during a dual generator failure, the inverters automatically revert from their respective generator bus to receive power from the center bus.

Volt/Frequency Meter

The volt/frequency meter, located on the overhead panel, indicates the frequency of the AC power being supplied to the avionics equipment. When the button on the lower left side of the meter is pressed, the AC voltage being supplied to the avionics equipment is indicated.

Limitations

Generator Limits

Maximum sustained generator load limit is as follows:

Generator Load %	Minimum Gas Generator RPM (% N_1)
0 to 75	65
75 to 100	72

Starter Limits

If ignition occurs within 20 seconds of any start attempt, there is no limit on the time the starter is engaged for that start.

For restarts following a normal start: 3 minute cool down, beginning when the starter is turned off.

For an aborted start (no ignition) followed by an attempted restart: Starter is limited to 20 seconds on (aborted start), 30 seconds off; 20 seconds on (second attempt), 60 seconds off; 20 seconds on (third start attempt), 5 minutes off.

For continuous motoring without attempting to start the engine: Starter is limited to 20 seconds on, 5 minutes off. Repeat as required.

Electrical System
Beech 1900D

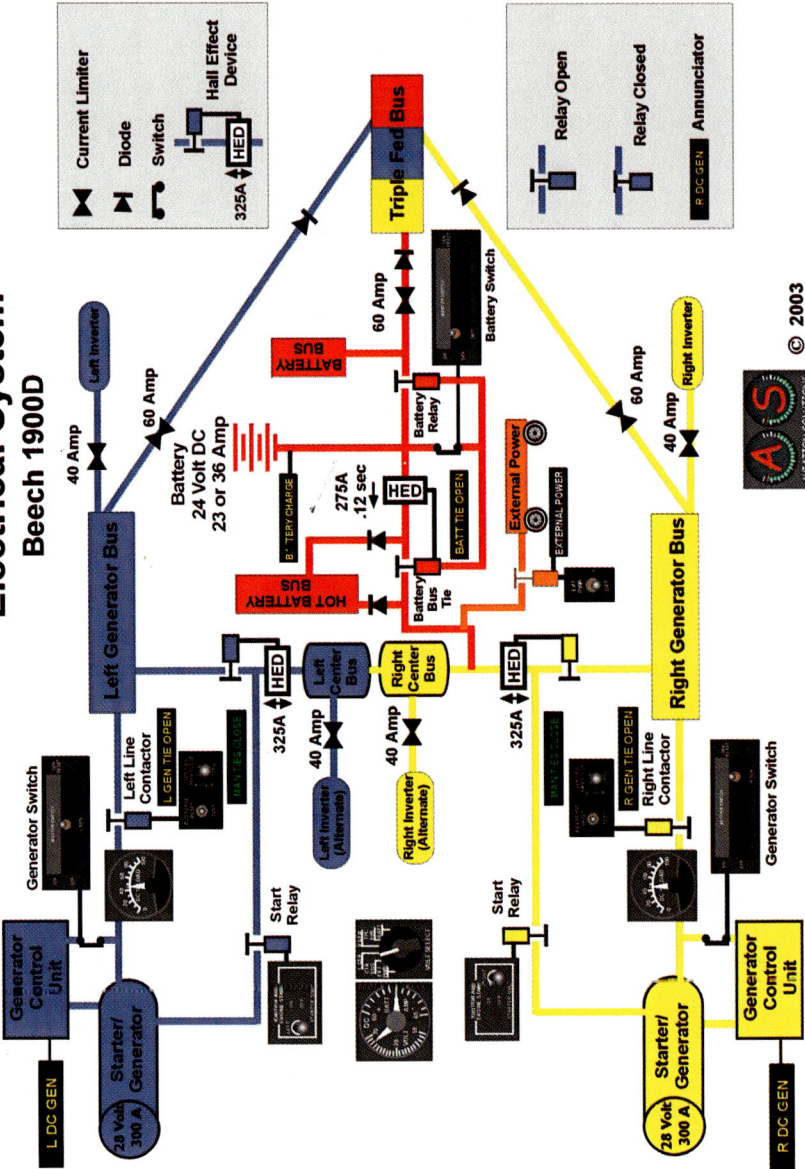

Legend (top left):
- Current Limiter
- Diode
- Switch
- Hall Effect Device
- 325A ⇅ HED

Legend (top right):
- Relay Open
- Relay Closed
- R DC GEN — Annunciator

Diagram labels:
- Left Inverter
- Right Inverter
- Triple Fed Bus
- Battery Switch
- 60 Amp
- 40 Amp
- BATTERY BUS
- Battery Relay
- Battery 24 Volt DC 23 or 36 Amp
- 275A .12 sec
- HED
- BATT TIE OPEN
- External Power
- EXTERNAL POWER
- HOT BATTERY BUS
- Battery Bus Tie
- Left Generator Bus
- Right Generator Bus
- Left Center Bus
- Right Center Bus
- 325A ⇅ HED
- 40 Amp
- Left Inverter (Alternate)
- Right Inverter (Alternate)
- Left Line Contactor
- Right Line Contactor
- L GEN TIE OPEN
- R GEN TIE OPEN
- Generator Switch
- Start Relay
- Generator Control Unit
- Starter/ Generator
- 28 Volt 300 A
- L DC GEN
- R DC GEN
- VOLT SELECT

AVIATION SOLUTIONS
© 2003

Chapter 7

LANDING GEAR AND BRAKES

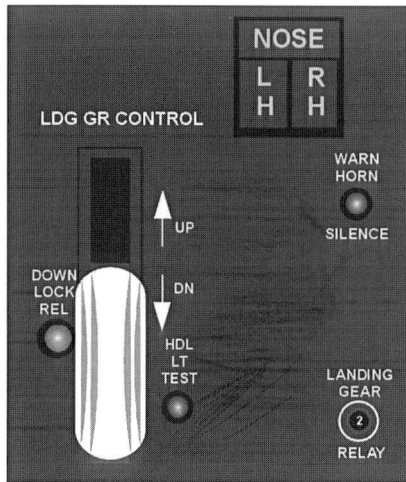

The components that make up the nose gear and both main gear are a shock strut, torque knee, trunion, drag brace, actuator, rollers and actuator cams. A control handle in the cockpit controls the gear electrically, and an independent hydraulic system actuates it. Gear position is indicated by six position lights, 4 green and two red.

A warning horn alerts the pilot if the gear is not down and locked and the aircraft is in the landing configuration. In case the primary hydraulic system fails, a manual system provides for backup gear extension.

Landing Gear Components

The shock strut is an air-oil type strut. The weight of the airplane rests on the compressed air in the strut. As weight is placed on the airplane, the lower portion of the strut moves into the upper portion, forcing the hydraulic fluid to increase the air pressure to cushion the weight. Normal extension of the main struts are 5.12 to 5.6 inches and the nose strut 5.25 to 5.75 inches, which means on the ground you should be able to see a little over 5 inches of the silver part of the strut. The upper portion of the strut is encased in a trunion, a triangular shaped metal piece connected to the aircraft structure.

The torque knee connects the trunion to the wheel shaft. It allows the shock strut to move up and down while resisting rotational forces, which keeps the wheels aligned with the longitudinal axis of the airplane.

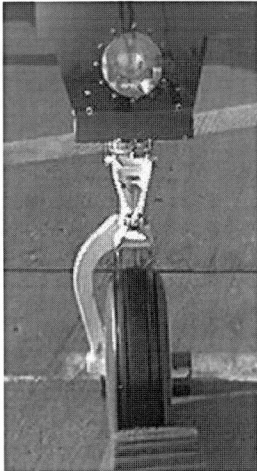

The actuator is like a piston that uses hydraulic fluid to move the drag brace to extend or retract the landing gear. An internal locking mechanism in the actuator holds the gear in the down and locked position. The drag brace is the rigid component of the gear. The upper end is connected to the aircraft structure and the lower end to the trunion. The drag brace is hinged in the middle so when the actuator moves it to a 2° overcenter position, it locks the gear in the down position.

The rollers are like metal screws attached to the base of the trunion. As the gear retracts, the rollers fit into actuating cams that move the gear doors closed. As the gear is extended, they roll out of the actuating cams and open the gear doors.

Nose Gear

The nose gear retracts aft into the wheel well. As the nose wheel retracts, a straightener roller centers the nose wheel and disconnects it from the rudder pedals. Along with the over-center positioning of the drag brace, a mechanical hook holds the nose wheel in the down and locked position. The tire is a tubeless 10-ply tire pressurized to 60 psi (+5/-0 psi).

Mounted above the nose gear is a taxi light. It is controlled in the cockpit from the overhead panel exterior light section. If the gear is retracted and the taxi light switch is left on a white [TAXI LIGHT] annunciator will illuminate.

Main Gear

The main landing gear retracts forward into the nacelle wheel wells. Each main gear has two tires and a brake assembly. The main gear tires are tubeless 10-ply pressurized to 97 psi (+5/-0 psi). The maximum true speed across the ground for the tires is 190 mph. This can become a concern at high elevation airports when true speeds are higher than indicated airspeeds.

Landing Gear Handle

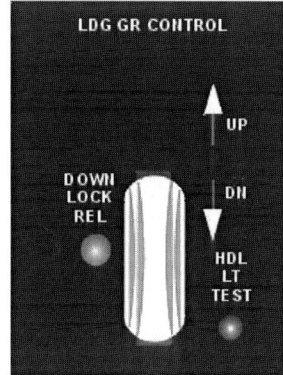

The landing gear handle is located on the right side of the pilot's subpanel. The gear handle must be pulled out of a detent to move it from the "UP" or "DOWN" position. There is a safety switch on the right main gear to prevent accidental gear retraction while on the ground. When there is weight on the safety switch, the landing gear control circuit is opened and a mechanical latch hook is activated to hold the gear handle down. If the safety switch does not accurately sense the aircraft in flight, this hook can be manually released by pushing on the red DOWN LOCK REL button located to the left of the control handle.

Hydraulic Extension and Retraction

There are three hydraulic lines that are used for gear extension and retraction. Two are for extension (one for normal operations and the second for manual gear extension) and one for retraction. Engine bleed air is plumbed into the hydraulic reservoir to prevent landing gear pump cavitation.

When the landing gear handle is placed in the "UP" position, electrical power is supplied to the gear selector valve and the hydraulic pump motor. The gear selector valve routes hydraulic fluid to the retract side of the actuators. 375 psi of hydraulic pressure to the actuators is necessary before the landing gear will unlock and retract. Hydraulic fluid contained in the extend side of the system returns to the reservoir through the normal extend plumbing. The landing gear motor is protected with a 60 amp circuit breaker that is not accessible in the cockpit. A 2 amp circuit breaker is located next to the gear handle, which protects the control circuit to the pump motor.

When the gear is up, the gear doors cover the top braces of the main gear while the lower portion of the wheels remain exposed in the airflow. The landing gear is held in the "UP" position by hydraulic pressure. An accumulator precharged to 800 psi takes the pressure bumps out of the system and assists in holding the gear up. When 2775 psi is reached, a pressure switch shuts off power to the pump motor. The same pressure switch activates the pump motor if hydraulic pressure drops below approximately 2320 psi. During gear retraction or extension, the motor will shut off if it operates more than $16 \pm .5$ seconds.

Placing the landing gear handle "DOWN" causes the gear to extend by energizing the pump motor that provides hydraulic fluid to the extend side of the landing gear actuators. The hydraulic fluid contained in the retract side of the system flows through the normal retract plumbing and into the hydraulic reservoir. When the actuators are fully extended, a ball is placed in the grooved portion of the gear actuator, and when the drag brace moves into the over-center locking position, it makes contact with a micro switch that satisfies the light requirement and tells the pump to shut off.

If the hydraulic fluid drops below a preset value in the landing gear reservoir a caution [HYD FLUID LOW] annunciator illuminates in the cockpit. There still should be enough hydraulic fluid left to extend the gear normally, but the hydraulic fluid level should be visually checked after arriving at your next destination. The dipstick for the reservoir is located on the left wing between the engine nacelle and fuselage.

There is a limitation on the frequency of landing gear cycles to ensure pump motor cooling. The first three cycles require 2 minutes between each cycle. Each cycle after three requires 5 minutes cooling time.

Position Indicators

Six landing gear position lights, four green and two red, indicate the position of the landing gear. The four green lights illuminate whenever the landing gear is down and locked (one light each for the LH and RH and two for the nose). There are two micro switches in each gear that need to be satisfied to illuminate the green light. One switch is satisfied when the actuator locks the gear in place, and the other is when the drag brace reaches the overcenter position. The green lights get their power from the triple fed bus, so if for some reason this is not receiving power, the lights will not illuminate. The green lights can be tested by pressing the annunciator test switch located to the

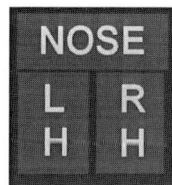

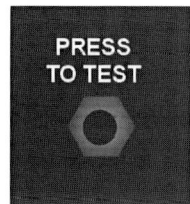

right of the warning annunciators. A special tool is required to remove and change the landing gear bulbs with other annunciator bulbs.

The two red lights inside the clear landing gear control handle illuminate to indicate the gear is in transit or when either of the micro switches does not agree with the landing gear handle position. All of the lights are extinguished when the landing gear is up and locked. The red lights in the gear handle can be tested by pressing the "HDL LT TEST" button next to the gear handle.

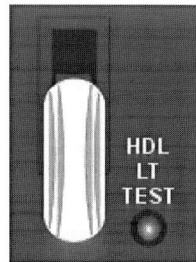

Warning Horn

As a safety reminder, there are two micro switches that cause a warning horn to sound if either or both power levers are reduced below approximately 84% to 86% N_1 or 1/3 quadrant travel with the landing gear not down and locked. This condition will also illuminate the red lights in the landing gear handle. The horn will also sound when the flaps are extended beyond the 17° position with the gear up. With the flaps up or in the 17° position, the horn can be silenced by pressing the button placarded WARN HORN SILENCE located to the right of the landing gear handle.

Manual Extension

You can manually extend the landing gear by using the emergency pump handle located to the right of the pilot's seat. To execute manual extension, the landing gear control handle must be in the down position, the LANDING GEAR RELAY circuit breaker located to the right of the gear control handle must be pulled, and airspeed must be below 180 knots. Due to gravity and the weight of the gear, it will fall within one inch of fully extended.

Removing the emergency pump handle from its spring clip and pumping up and down draws hydraulic fluid from the secondary reservoir, through the emergency extend plumbing, to the extend side of the actuator. The hydraulic fluid in the retract side of the actuator will flow through the normal retract plumbing into the primary reservoir. It takes approximately 80 strokes to get the gear locked down. If the electrical system is operative, the landing gear may be checked for full down with the gear position lights. When the gear down lights illuminate, stop pumping and stow the handle.

If for some reason the gear does not indicate down and locked, continue pumping until sufficient resistance is felt to be sure that the gear is down and locked. Because the emergency pump handle is located next to the captain's seat, it would be advisable to let the copilot land while the captain continues to pump hydraulic fluid into the system until the aircraft is safely up on jacks. To prevent gear retraction on the ground after emergency extension, do not move any landing gear controls or reset any switches or circuit breakers until the malfunction has been determined and corrected.

It would be an indication that the gear is not down and locked and not an indication problem if any of the following conditions exist.

- Red light illuminated in the handle
- Gear down annunciator is not illuminated, but does illuminate when testing the lights.
- Gear warning horn sounds when power lever retarded or flaps selected beyond approach.

If several of the following items occur the problem would seem to be an indication problem in the gear system.

- The GPWS does not give a "TOO LOW GEAR" aual alert when below 500 feet AGL and below 148 knots, if installed.
- Red light in the handle is not illuminated.
- No gear warning horn when power levers are retarded or flaps are selected beyond appraoch.
- Gear down annunciator does not illuminate when testing the lights.

Brakes

Both main gear are equipped with dual multi-disc hydraulic brakes. Each toe pedal has its own master cylinder. Braking action happens when hydraulic pressure is applied to five small pistons in the brake housing. Either pilot can apply pressure to help stop the aircraft.

Hydraulic fluid for the brakes is stored in a container in the right side avionics nose compartment. This fluid is routed in a series through the pilots master cylinders.

The parking brake handle is located in the center pedestal. There are two parking brake check valves that trap hydraulic pressure in the lines to the brakes. Each side has its own valves, and setting the parking brake closes both valves. To set the parking brake, pump the brake pedals to increase pressure in the brake line and pull up on the parking brake handle.

The parking brake is a temporary means of holding the aircraft's position until you move or until chocks are placed around the tires. The brake lines are not protected from thermal expansion. Brakes normally reach their maximum temperature about 15 minutes after landing. If you set the parking brake and the brakes continue to heat up, the fluid expands, and if trapped by the parking brake, can cause damage and make it difficult to release the parking brake.

Anti-skid

The brakes are protected with an anti-skid system that is turned on with a switch on the pedestal. The anti-skid control box monitors wheel speed, and as one wheel approaches a skid it will release hydraulic pressure to maintain the wheels at maximum effectiveness while preventing them from locking up.

An electrically driven pump increases hydraulic pressure to the anti-skid system. An accumulator is also part of the system to remove pressure bumps and to store enough pressure for 10 brake applications in the event of a pump motor failure. The [ANTI SKID FAIL] annunciator alerts you if there is an electrical fault or low hydraulic pressure and anti-skid protection is not available.

Since the anti-skid system regulates hydraulic pressure to brakes during maximum braking conditions, traditional differential braking for steering is not available. Directional control can be maintained with nose wheel steering, or you can reduce the pedal force on the opposite toe brake as what direction you want the airplane to go.

Power Steering

Power steering is an optional accessory on the 1900. It is a electrically controlled and hydraulically actuated system. The hydraulic actuator, located above the nose gear strut, uses fluid from the brake reservoir.

There are two modes it can operate in, park and taxi. In the taxi mode the nose wheel can turn ± 15° of center and in the park mode much tighter turns are possible at ± 55°. When turned on with the switch on the pedestal, "POWER ON", a green [PWR STEER ENGA] annunciator will illuminate indicating the system is operating.

The system is not meant to be used for the takeoff roll. The system will automatically turn off, and default to the taxi mode, once the power levers are moved above 89 to 91% N_1. If you attempt to turn the power steering off with the switch and the system does not disengage, a yellow [MAN STEER FAIL] annunciator will illuminate. This indicates the nose wheel will not move freely with rudder pedal movement and is still under control of the power steering system. If the power steering system has also failed the nose wheel will remain where it was when the system failed.

A yellow [PWR STEER FAIL] annunciator will illuminate when hydraulic pressure is low or there is an electrical failure in the power steering system. If the hydraulic pressure is low the system will operate sluggishly, while if it was an electrical failure the system will turn off.

Switching between the park and taxi modes should be done while stopped or while moving very slowly. Immediate movement of the nose wheel occurs if the rudder pedals are not centered.

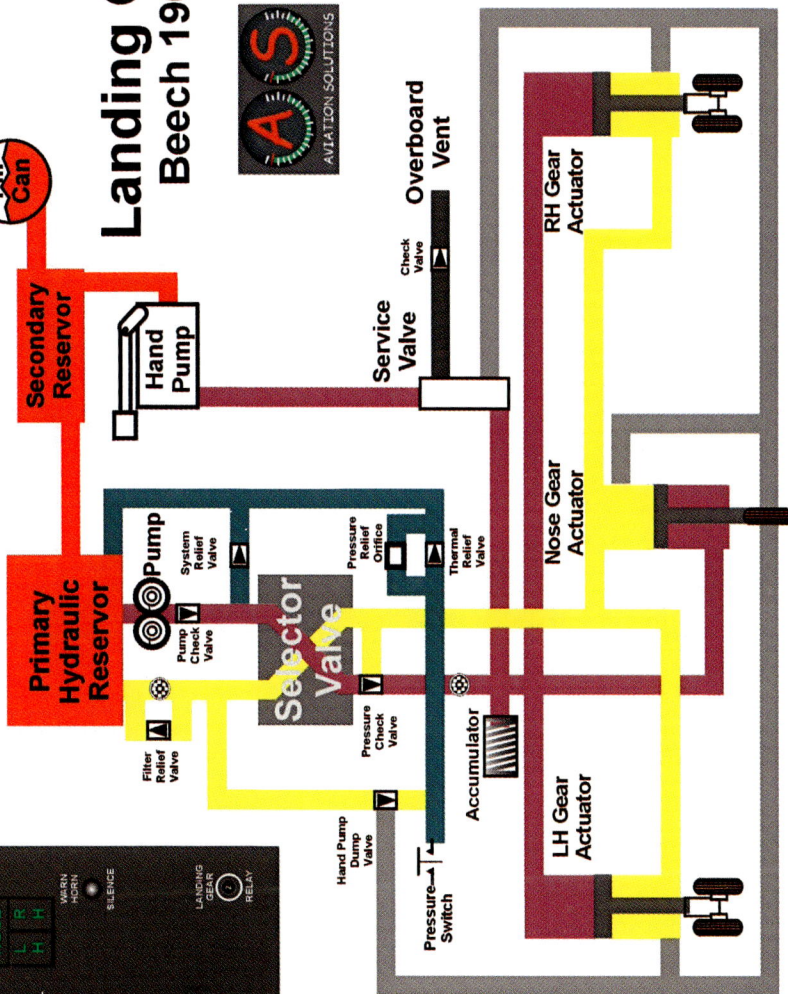

Landing Gear
Beech 1900D

© 2003

Bleed Air

Fill Can

Secondary Reservor

Hand Pump

Primary Hydraulic Reservor

Pump

System Relief Valve

Pump Check Valve

Filter Relief Valve

Selector Valve

Pressure Check Valve

Service Valve

Check Valve

Overboard Vent

Pressure Relief Orifice

Thermal Relief Valve

Hand Pump Dump Valve

Accumulator

Pressure Switch

RH Gear Actuator

Nose Gear Actuator

LH Gear Actuator

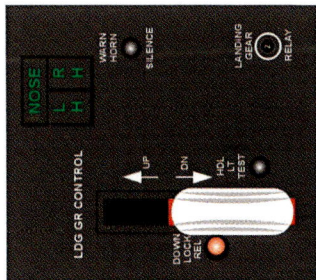

LDG GR CONTROL

UP / DN

DOWN LOCK REL

HDL LT TEST

NOSE
L   R
H   H

WARN HORN

SILENCE

LANDING GEAR

RELAY

Notes:

Chapter 8

ENVIRONMENTAL

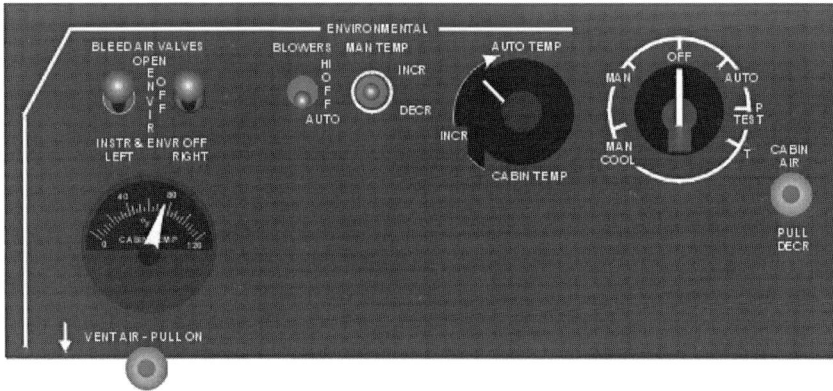

The first officer is considered the environmental specialist because he/she operates the temperature control and pressurization systems. The environmental system includes temperature control, pressurization, and pneumatic and vacuum systems. Bleed air is used to power the entire environmental system. The environmental diagram included in the back of this chapter can be broken down into two main sections. The lower half of the diagram is the temperature control and pressurization. The upper half is the pneumatic and vacuum part of the environmental system.

Bleed Air

Bleed air (P_3) is the force behind the whole environmental system and is taken from the compressor section of each engine. At a takeoff power setting, bleed air comes off the engine at a temperature of 800°F and is routed to five different locations.

- Brake de-ice (described in detail in ice protection chapter)
- Fuel control unit (part of fuel system - not shown on diagram)
- P_3 purge tank (part of fuel system - not shown on diagram)
- Precooler heat exchange
- Bypass valve

From the engine, bleed air flows through a precooler heat exchanger, then flows to both portions of the environmental system (pressurization, temperature control and pneumatic, vacuum). For pressurization and temperature control, the precooler air mixes with the bleed air that does not get cooled from the bypass valve to get a temperature of 450° ± 25° F. The mixed air for the temperature control and pressurization is regulated to 38 ± 2 psi. The air from the precooler that goes to the pneumatic and vacuum part of the environmental system is regulated to 18 psi.

Bleed Air Valve Switches

Two bleed air valve switches located on the copilot's left subpanel control bleed air flow. With the bleed air valves open, all environmental systems are receiving bleed air. With both switches in the "ENVIR OFF" position, only the pneumatic and vacuum systems (upper portion of the diagram) are receiving bleed air. When the bleed air switch is placed in the "ENVIR OFF" position a white [L or R ENVIR OFF] annunciator will illuminate.

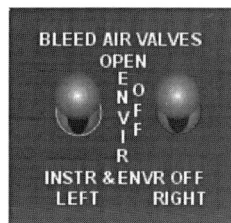

With both switches in the "INST & ENVIR OFF" position, nothing is receiving bleed air. The switches are powered open from the electrical system. If there was a complete electrical failure, the environmental bleed air valves would close, and the cabin pressure would slowly leak down. The instrument bleed air valves remain open in the event of a complete electrical failure.

Pressurization

The pressurization system takes ambient air and increases its pressure to eliminate the need for supplemental oxygen. This creates a positive pressure from the inside of the cabin pushing outward. The aircraft is not designed to withstand negative pressure from the outside in. Only the cabin needs to be pressurized for pilot and passenger comfort. The wings, tail, and nose cone do not need to be pressurized. For this reason there is a "Pressure Vessel" that extends from in front of the cockpit to just aft of the baggage compartment that is pressurized. There are wires and cables that pass through the pressure vessel to unpressurized parts of the airplane that cannot be completely sealed. Therefore, there is continuously a slow leak of air out of the pressure vessel. The leak is minimized with rubber seals that inflate with bleed air around the doors.

Engine bleed air that passes through the temperature control (lower half of the diagram) is used to pressurize the airplane. The bleed air provides a maximum pressure differential of 5.1 ± .1 psi between the pressure vessel and the outside air. This pressure differential provides a sea level cabin pressure altitude up to approximately 11,000 feet, and an approximate 9000 foot cabin altitude with the aircraft at 25,000 feet. At altitudes between 11,000 and 25,000 feet, the cabin altitude varies between sea level and 9000 feet.

To alert the pilots if the cabin pressurizes to much, a [CABIN DIFF HI] annunciator illuminates when the cabin pressure differential exceeds 5.25 psi.

Pressurization Controller

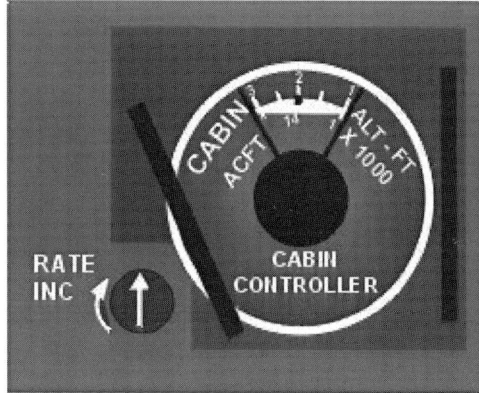

The cabin pressurization controller controls the pressurization of the cabin and the rate of pressure changes. An adjustable dual-scale indicator dial (shown at right) is used to select the desired cabin pressure altitude. The outer scale indicates the cabin pressure altitude. The inner scale indicates the maximum altitude the airplane can climb to without exceeding the maximum pressure differential.

Rotating the knob in the center of the controller will set both scales. The rate of cabin pressure change is adjusted with the small knob to the lower left of the dial. It is adjustable between approximately 200 and 2000 feet per minute (fpm).

Pressurization Indication

Actual cabin altitude and pressure differential are constantly indicated by a cabin altimeter located on a panel forward of the control pedestal. The large needle indicates the cabin altitude in thousands of feet and the small needle indicates the pressure

---

ENVIRONMENTAL   79 differential between the pressure vessel and ambient air. Cabin vertical speed is displayed to the left of the cabin altimeter and functions much like the aircraft's vertical speed indicator, but it indicates cabin rate of climb and descent rather than the aircraft's rate of climb and descent.

Cabin Differential Pressure Limitations

Approved Operating Range (Green Arc)   0 to 5.1 psi
Unapproved Operating Range (Red Arc)   above 5.1 psi

Outflow Valve

Air is always flowing into the cabin at a rate of between 8 and 16 pounds per minute, depending on pressure altitude and temperature. There are two vacuum-operated outflow valves to vent the excess air that the pressurization system does not need. The outflow valve controls cabin pressure and rate of cabin pressure change by regulating the amount of air allowed to escape from the aircraft. The outflow valves are located in the rear of the pressure vessel (in the baggage compartment) and air is vented overboard to prevent moisture from accumulating in the baggage compartment. A landing gear safety switch on the left main gear triggers maximum vacuum to the outflow valves, pulling them full open when the aircraft is on the ground to prevent the aircraft from being pressurized on the ground. If the cabin was pressurized and the airstair door was opened, it would explode open, injuring the operator and damaging the aircraft. Negative pressure relief comes from the design of the spring in the outflow valve. If the pressure outside the cabin is higher than that of the inside pressure, the air pushes the valves open.

Poppet Valve

A part of the outflow valve is called a poppet valve, which provides maximum positive pressure differential relief. The poppet valve lets air escape from the cabin when pressure exceeds 5.1 psi. There are two static ports located on the aft pressure bulkhead that compare cabin air to outside air to determine the pressure differential. The static ports are plumbed to the poppet valve, and when the outside pressure reaches the preset differential, the high pressure inside the cabin will push against the outflow valve toward the low pressure causing the outflow valve to open and allow the high pressure out.

Cabin Pressure Switch

A cabin pressure switch allows the pilot to fly pressurized or unpressurized and test the system. When the switch is set in the center "PRESS" position, the cabin pressurization controller adjusts the outflow valve, allowing the cabin to pressurize. When the switch is placed forward in the "DUMP" position, maximum vacuum is applied to the outflow valve, allowing the cabin to depressurize and/or remain unpressurized. In the "TEST" position, the landing gear safety switch is bypassed, holding the outflow valve in the closed position, which permits testing of the pressurization system during ground operation. To test on the ground, place the bleed air valve switches in the "OPEN" position, set the cabin altitude selector to 1000 feet below the field pressure altitude, and with the cabin rate control knob set at the 12 o'clock position, hold the cabin pressure switch to the "TEST" position. The cabin vertical speed indicator should then indicate a decent. It may take up to one minute before a descent is indicated.

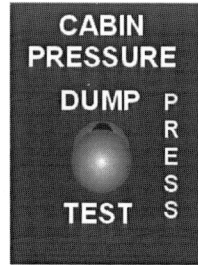

Operation

Prior to takeoff, set the aircraft altitude selector to 1000 feet above the planned cruise altitude to prevent the pressurization system from experiencing "bumps," which are fluctuations in cabin pressure that cause your ears to pop. They are caused when the aircraft's altitude exceeds the altitude set on the pressurization controller. The extra 1000 feet gives you a margin to work with in case you experience turbulence that upsets your altitude or if the pressurization controller is out of adjustment. Also, set the rate knob to the 12 o'clock position, which gives an approximate 500 fpm rate of climb or descent.

If you change to a new cruise altitude in flight, reset the cabin altitude knob to 1000 feet above your new altitude. Prior to descent, you should set the selector to 500 feet above the field pressure altitude to ensure that the aircraft is landed unpressurized. If the aircraft is landed pressurized, the outflow valve will open and equalize the pressure at a rate of 6000 fpm which could cause damage to your ears.

Altitude Warning

A pressure sensing switch, located on the forward pressure bulkhead, will cause a [CABIN ALT HI] annunciator to illuminate if the cabin altitude exceeds 10,000 feet.

Temperature Control

In addition to pressurization, the environmental system also heats and cools cabin air and provides fresh air ventilation. Automatic and manual controls for heating and cooling are located on the copilot's left subpanel.

The lower half of the diagram in the back of this chapter displays the heating and cooling function of the environmental system. Engine bleed air is cooled to 450° ± 25°F and regulated to 38 ± 2 psi by mixing air that is either sent through a precooler or directly to the environmental system. The air is mixed by the movement of two valves opening or closing to get the proper temperature of 450°.

Then the air flows to two places to further regulate the temperature, an air cycle machine (ACM) or through the ACM bypass valve. For maximum heating, the ACM bypass valve is completely open, allowing the bleed air to flow through an ejector, which partially cools the air, and then into the cabin through the floor vents. For maximum cooling the ACM bypass valve closes and the air passes through the air cycle machine, which cools it to 15° below the ambient temperature. For temperatures in-between, the airflow is regulated between going through the ACM and the bypass valve so they mix to get the appropriate temperature.

The ACM uses the air that passes through it to power itself and incorporates two heat exchangers along with compressing and expanding the air to cool it. Once the air enters the ACM it flows through the first stage heat exchanger. The air then flows through a compressor that increases the pressure and temperature. The second stage heat exchanger further removes excess heat before the air flows through an expansion turbine, which reduces the pressure and temperature while providing the force necessary to operate the ACM compressor. A final ejector expands and further cools the air before it enters the cabin through the floor vents.

Part of the ACM is a vapor cycle machine (VCM) that can further cool the air to 25° below ambient temperature. The VCM is a freon air conditioner. When the air cycle machine is at maximum cooling and the ACM bypass valve is fully closed, the VCM is turned on. The VCM is powered from the right engine accessory gearbox.

Two systems are incorporated to keep the VCM compressor operation within limits. If freon pressure limits are exceeded (high or low), limit switches interrupt power to the compressor clutch and the condenser blower. Also, if the ambient air temperature is below 45 ± 5° F, the VCM will not operate. Air from the VCM enters the cabin through the eyeball outlets next to each seat. If the VCM is not on, recirculated air from the cabin flows through an evaporator then back into the cabin through the eyeball outlets.

When the cabin air cools below what you have selected, the ACM bypass valve begins to open. When the ACM bypass valve is completely open it sends a signal to the VCM to turn off.

Controlling Temperature From The Cockpit

The cabin temperature is controlled by a rotary type switch placarded OFF/AUTO/P TEST/T TEST/MAN COOL/MAN. The temperature can be controlled automatically or manually. In the auto mode, the cabin temp dial is rotated between cold and hot, and the system regulates the ACM bypass valve to maintain the selected temperature.

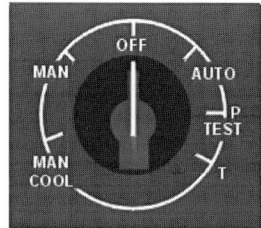

One thing to note is that there is always some air that will go through the ACM and then mix with the hotter air before entering the cabin.

In the manual mode, there is a switch that can be held up in the "INCREASE" or down in the "DECREASE" position to regulate temperature. As you hold the switch in the increase or decrease position, you are actually moving the ACM bypass valve. Changes in power will affect the amount of air flowing through the system. Therefore, if temperature is being regulated in the manual mode, to maintain a specific temperature you must adjust the valves every time there is a change in power setting.

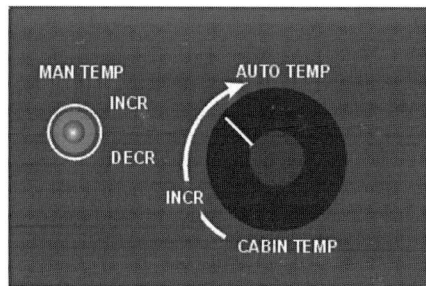

The ACM bypass valve takes 30 seconds to move from open to close. Therefore, while operating in either auto or manual mode, there is a time delay before you will feel a temperature change.

In manual cool mode, the ACM limit switch is bypassed and the VCM will run regardless of the ACM bypass valve position, as long as the ambient temperature is above 45° F and the right engine is running. It is not recommended to continuously operate

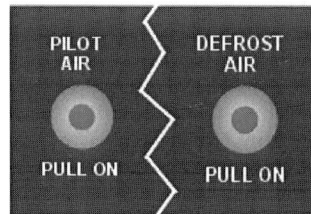

in the manual cool mode since it may cause ice formation in the ACM.

Push-pull knobs provide additional control of the environmental system. On the pilot's side there are knobs that increase or decrease the amount of airflow to the pilot and windshield defrost. The copilot has knobs that control airflow to the copilot and passenger cabin. When the pilot and copilot air knobs are pulled out, the maximum amount of airflow is allowed into the cockpit. With the cabin air knob pulled out, airflow to the cabin is minimized. The further the defrost air knob is pulled out, more air is directed to the cockpit windshields. If all the knobs are pulled out, there is maximum airflow to the cockpit; with all knobs in, there is maximum airflow to the cabin.

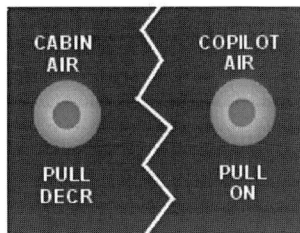

Temperature and Pressure Limits

The warning [L or R BL AIR FAIL] annunciator will illuminate when either the temperature or pressure sensor indicate that $500 \pm 25°$ F or 44 psi has been exceeded. When this happens, the environmental shut off valve, precooler bypass, and through valve will automatically close and the advisory [L or R ENVIR OFF] annunciator will illuminate. The memory procedure is to bring the bleed air valve switch to the "ENVIR OFF" position then back "OPEN." If the warning environmental fail annunciator does not illuminate again when you bring the switch to open, you know that it was just a transient surge of air that set off either the temperature or pressure sensor.

Test Functions

The over temperature and over pressure protection circuits can be tested in the "P TEST" and "T TEST" positions of the mode controller, respectively.

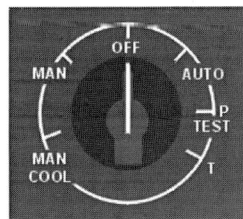

The P TEST will test an over pressure condition. It is usually only done by maintenance. Power must be above 80% N_1 for at least 30 to 45 seconds. The [L and R BL AIR FAIL] and [L and R ENVIR OFF] annunciators should illuminate, indicating the system was shutdown.

The T TEST will test an over temperature condition. This test is normally done by the pilots before the first flight of the day. The [L and

R BL AIR FAIL] and [L and R ENVIR OFF] annunciators should illuminate immediately after the T TEST is selected. Switch the bleed air valves to instrument and environmental off then back open to reset the system.

Unpressurized Ventilation

A ram air scoop, located on the forward right nose section, supplies outside air to the cabin. To allow the air to flow into the cabin the vent air knob, located on the copilots left subpanel, must be pulled open. The ram air system is designed to provide ambient air into the aircraft while unpressurized. To remain unpressurized, the cabin pressure switch must be in the dump position. A spring holds the valve open when the aircraft is unpressurized. During pressurized operation, cabin pressure holds the valve closed along with a solenoid connected to the pressurization dump switch. While the aircraft is unpressurized, you can still operate with the bleed air valves open to supplement the ambient air, or they can be off to use ambient air only. The ram air enters the cabin through the floor vents and is recirculated through the eyeball outlets.

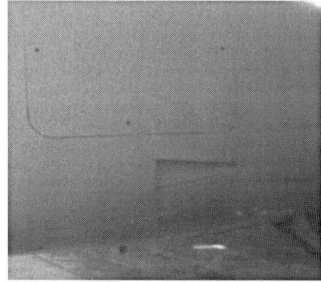

VENT AIR - PULL ON

CABIN
PRESSURE
DUMP   P
       R
       E
       S
TEST   S

Ventilation Blower

The ventilation blower, located in the lower nose section forward of the copilot's rudder pedals, recirculates the cabin air by drawing it forward and forcing it through the air conditioner evaporator into the mixing plenum. The mixing plenum is divided into two sections; one supplies conditioned air to the overhead ducts and side wall eyeball outlets, and the other supplies heated air to the floor vents. The switch that controls the ventilation blower is located on the copilot's left subpanel with other environmental controls. With the switch you may select the "HI," "OFF" or "AUTO" position. When the switch is placed in the "AUTO" position, the vent blower runs as long as the mode controller is on anything but off. In the high (HI) position, it runs at that speed regardless of the mode controller position.

BLOWERS
HI
O
F
F
AUTO

For normal operations the switch is left is the "HI" position which allows airflow through the cabin even when the mode controller is turned off for takeoff. In aircraft with serial number UE 2-6 has a "LOW" position on the vent blower which was replaced with the "OFF" position in UE 7 and after.

Pneumatic and Vacuum

The upper portion of the diagram shows the pneumatic and vacuum systems. Bleed air is supplied at a pressure of 90 to 150 psi from both engines and is regulated down to 18 ± 1 psi. With only one engine running, there is sufficient pressure to operate all the pneumatic and vacuum systems. There is a check valve that does not allow reverse airflow from one engine to go to the pneumatic and vacuum systems then leak out the opposite engine valve. There is a 21 psi relief valve that protects the system from overpressure. The pneumatic pressure gauge should read 18 psi during normal operation (green arc 17-20 psi).

Pneumatic

Pneumatic pressure is used for 5 items:

- Bleed air warning
- Landing gear hydraulic fill can
- Surface de-ice
- Pressure switch for the Hobbs meter
- Venturi to run the vacuum system.

In addition to the bleed air being regulated to 18 psi for the pneumatic system, it is also cooled to 70° F above outside air temperature. Unlike the pressurization system, the instrument air valve is spring loaded to the open position. If all electrical power is lost, the valve remains open, and the pneumatic systems operate normally. Only one engine bleed air supply is required to fully operate the entire pneumatic system.

During the engine start process, you don't want to allow any of the air in the engine to escape, to allow maximum air cooling in the burner can. To prevent from air coming out of the engine during start and entering the pneumatic and other systems, all of the bleed air lines have a 4 psi restrictor on them. This keeps air in the engine until pressure is built up that ensures sufficient air is available for cooling. Once there is over 4 psi of pressure in the line, airflow is allowed to the pneumatic system.

If a bleed air line were to rupture, it has the potential to damage adjacent aircraft wiring, tubing, or the aircraft skin because of the heat associated with engine bleed air. For bleed air line rupture warning, plastic ethylene vinyl acetate (EVA) tubing is wrapped around all the bleed air lines and is pressurized to 18 psi from the pneumatic system. In the event of a bleed air line rupture, the hot air would melt the plastic EVA tubing, causing the pressure in the EVA line to decrease below 1 psi, which would illuminate a [L or R BL AIR FAIL] annunciator light. This would be an indication to the pilot to immediately shut off the associated bleed air valve. The annunciator will remain illuminated even with the bleed air valve off because the ruptured tubing is no longer able to remain pressurized to 18 psi. The only way to repair this is to replace the tubing.

The landing gear hydraulic fill can is pressurized to prevent pump cavitation (keeps bubbles out of hydraulic fluid and increases pump life). The Hobbs meter only runs when in the air (sensed by the left landing gear squat switch), the flap circuit breaker is in, and when the pressure switch is satisfied.

Pneumatic pressure is also used to inflate the rubber de-ice boots on the wing and tail for surface de-ice protection. The vacuum section of this chapter and ice protection chapter goes into more detail on how the pneumatic pressure it used operate the surface de-ice system.

Vacuum

The power for the vacuum system is provided by pneumatic pressure running through a venturi and creating a low pressure vacuum in the center of it. Vacuum pressure is used by the de-ice boots, pressurization controller, and gyro instruments.

The de-ice distributor valve is the brains of the surface de-ice. It uses vacuum pressure to hold the de-ice boots to the leading edge. Also, when selected by the pilot, it runs the surface de-ice through a cycle of using pneumatic pressure to inflate the boot to brake the ice off, and then uses vacuum pressure to bring the de-ice boot back in and hold it to the leading edge.

The vacuum regulator is used to supply the correct amount of suction as needed by the pressurization system (pressurization controller, outflow and safety valves) and the gyro instruments (attitude indicator and DG). The gyro suction gauge takes its reading just

VACUUM
INCHES OF MECURY

prior to the vacuum regulator [narrow green arc (normal operating range 15,000 - 30,000 feet) 3.0 to 4.3 inches Hg, green arc (normal operating range sea level - 15,000 feet) 4.3 to 5.9 inches Hg].

Environmental System
Beech 1900D

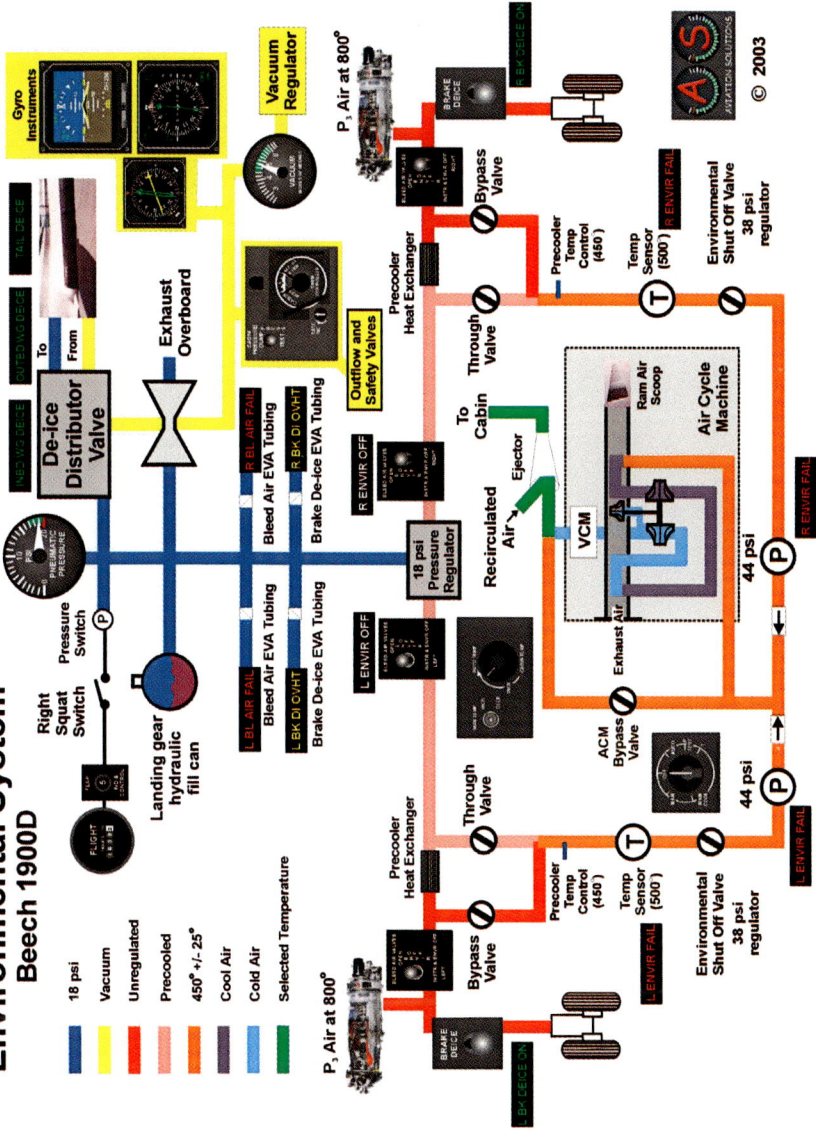

Legend:
- 18 psi
- Vacuum
- Unregulated
- Precooled
- 450° +/- 25°
- Cool Air
- Cold Air
- Selected Temperature

Gyro Instruments

Vacuum Regulator

Exhaust Overboard

De-ice Distributor Valve

Outflow and Safety Valves

Precooler Heat Exchanger

Pressure Switch

Right Squat Switch

Landing gear hydraulic fill can

L BL AIR FAIL — Bleed Air EVA Tubing
L BK DI OVHT — Brake De-ice EVA Tubing
R BL AIR FAIL — Bleed Air EVA Tubing
R BK DI OVHT — Brake De-ice EVA Tubing

18 psi Pressure Regulator

Recirculated Air

To Cabin

Ejector

VCM

Ram Air Scoop

Air Cycle Machine

Exhaust Air

Through Valve

ACM Bypass Valve

44 psi

44 psi

R ENVIR FAIL

L ENVIR FAIL

Precooler Temp Control (450°)

Temp Sensor (500°)

Environmental Shut Off Valve 38 psi regulator

Bypass Valve

Brake De-ice

P₃ Air at 800°

BK DE-ICE ON

© 2003

Notes:

ENVIRONMENTAL

Chapter 9

FUEL

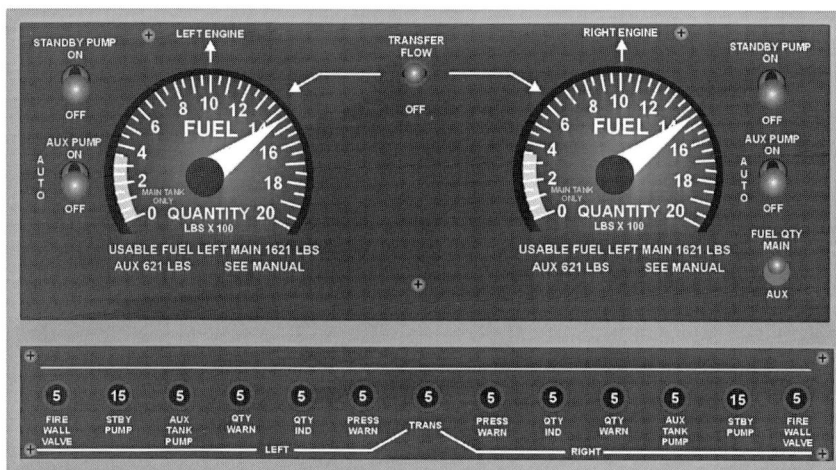

665.4 gallons (4484 pounds @ 6.74 pounds/gallon) of usable fuel is stored in the wings. In intermediate cruise at international standard atmosphere (ISA) conditions, fuel burn is approximately 800 pounds per hour at 15,000 feet, therefore with one hour of reserve the 1900 can fly about four and 1/☐ hours if filled to capacity.

Fuel Tanks

Each wing can hold 240.5 gallons in the main tanks and 92.2 gallons in the auxiliary tanks. The main tanks are located from the engine nacelle outward to the wing tip. The auxiliary tanks are located on the opposite side of the engine nacelle inward to the fuselage.

The collector tank is part of the main tank system, located immediately outboard of the nacelle, and is the distribution point for fuel going to the engine. This tank is submerged inside the main tank in the wing. It holds approximately 6 gallons of fuel and is used to provide air free fuel to the engine. Since the collector tank is where fuel is drawn from to go to the engine, to ensure it is always full the collector tank receives fuel six different ways:

- two jet transfer pumps
- main tank gravity fed through a series of flapper doors
- fuel pump in the auxiliary tank
- cross transfer line
- spillage from the main tank

There are two filler caps on each wing, one located between the engine nacelle and the fuselage for the auxiliary tank, and the other outboard the nacelle for the main tank. All filler ports have anti-siphon devices to prevent a loss of fuel if the fuel cap is not properly secured.

Fuel Movement

Follow along with the fuel system diagram at the back of this chapter as it is referenced to describe fuel movement from the tanks to the engine.

Fuel is moved using three boost pumps and three jet pumps. A boost pump can either be electrically powered or engine driven. Jet pumps do not require any electrical power to operate. A jet pump is a fuel line that is narrower in the middle than at the ends, and due to Bernoulli's principle, this creates a low pressure (vacuum) in the center of the line due to the increase in fuel velocity. Two fuel lines are attached in the middle where the vacuum is created. Each line draws fuel from either the main tank or collector tank and delivers it through the jet pump to the fuel manifold.

Jet pumps require a minimum amount of fuel movement through them to create enough vacuum to operate efficiently. To ensure this minimum flow through the main tank jet pump, the fuel system has a motive flow line. Motive flow is just fuel running under pressure that returns to the fuel tanks through the main tank jet pump. To get the whole system going, there is a standby electric boost pump that gets powered during the start process that begins the flow trough the fuel lines and back through the motive flow line to get the jet pump operating. Once sufficient flow is achieved and the engine is at idle speed, the standby boost pump turns off and the jet pump provides fuel to the engine driven boost pumps.

There are three jet pumps:

- Forward transfer jet pump
- Aft transfer jet pump
- Main tank jet pump

The manifold, located in the collector tank, is where the three jet pumps all route fuel to. The manifold is much like a jet pump in that when fuel from the motive flow line runs through the manifold, it creates the suction pressure to move fuel through the forward and aft transfer jet pumps. From the manifold, fuel is routed through two fuel shut off valves, a fuel filter and drain, then to an engine driven boost pump. The engine-driven boost pump (45 psi) increases the pressure of the fuel and provides fuel to two places, to the main tank jet pump through the motive flow fuel line and to the engine-driven high pressure boost pump.

After passing through the oil to fuel heat exchanger, the engine-driven high pressure boost pump (850 psi) gives the fuel the necessary pressure to reach the engine. If this fuel pump fails, so does the engine. In the upper left corner of the fuel system diagram, there is a minimum pressure flow valve. This valve is set to 100 psi. When the pressure drops below 100 psi, this valve closes, and fuel cannot reach the engine. Besides the 850 psi boost pump, the only other fuel pumps are 45 psi and 11 psi. Neither of these can boost the pressure enough to open the minimum pressure flow valve and send fuel to the engine.

Excess fuel that the fuel control unit does not need to operate the engine at the requested engine speed is returned to the fuel tank through the purge line. The purge line draws the excess fuel from the fuel line after the engine driven high pressure boost pump.

The fuel control unit distributes the proper amount of fuel to set the engine speed. It takes input from the power and condition lever setting, N_1 and the fuel topping governor. The fuel topping governor monitors N_2 and decreases the amount of fuel to the engine to control propeller rpm in certain cases when the primary propeller governor fails. For more information on propeller governors, see Chapter 5. Bypassing the fuel control unit is a minimum flow adjustment valve. This ensures a fuel flow of 90 pounds per hour (idle power) regardless of what the fuel control unit does.

Next in sequence after the fuel control unit is the fuel shut off valve, which is controlled by the condition lever in the cockpit. This is one of three fuel shut off valves, two which the pilot has control over. The other shut off valve the pilot has control over is the firewall fuel shut off valve (T-handle in the cockpit located above

FIRE PULL

the center pedestal on the instrument panel). In addition to shutting off fuel, the T-handle (labeled "FIRE PULL") will also arm the fire bottle on that engine. The only shut off valve the pilot does not have control over is the maintenance fuel shut off valve. The maintenance and firewall fuel shut off valves are located between the fuel manifold and the 45 psi engine driven boost pump. Once the firewall fuel valve is closed a yellow [L or R FW VALVE] annunciator illuminates in the cockpit.

The fuel flow gauge is between the condition lever fuel shut off valve and the minimum pressure flow valve. In sequence after the minimum pressure flow valve is the flow divider, which evenly distributes fuel between the primary and secondary fuel nozzles. The P_3 purge tank uses P_3 air from the engine to burn off excess fuel in the fuel nozzles and the fuel line to the engine after shutdown. The purge tank is pressurized to 100 psi, and when fuel pressure drops below 100 psi the purge tank blows hot P_3 air through the fuel nozzles and the engine. As a result, a momentary surge in N_1 should be observed after engine shutdown as the residual fuel is burned. The hot bleed air going through the combustion chamber causes white smoke to come out of the exhaust stacks when the bleed air meets the colder ambient air. This keeps the fuel lines free of fuel for two reasons; so it does not drip onto the ground and create environmental damage, and to help prevent fuel from being ignited too early in the start process and create a hot start.

Cavitation

Although the 850 psi high pressure boost pump delivers sufficient pressure by itself to run the engine, the high pressure creates cavitation around the pump. Cavitation occurs when a fluid in motion at a high pressure creates vapor pockets of air that form and collapse, which can cause damage to the pump. The 45 psi boost pump helps the fuel flow through the high pressure boost pump to prevent cavitation. If the 45 psi boost pump fails, there is a standby electric boost pump rated at 11 ± 2 psi to prevent cavitation. This pump is located in the collector tank and pushes fuel through the manifold. There is a switch on the fuel control panel to turn the standby fuel pump on.

Failure of the 45 psi boost pump is sensed by a 5 psi switch and indicated in the cockpit by a red [L or R FUEL PRES LO] annunciator.

Auxiliary Tank

Each auxiliary tank holds 92.2 gallons (618 pounds) of fuel. Fuel is moved from the auxiliary tank to the collector tank through the use of an auxiliary fuel pump. The control for the pump is on the fuel control

panel. With the switch in the auto position, the
pump will run until one of three conditions are
met:

- Float switch senses empty tank (Like one
  in a toilet bowl). When the auxiliary tank
  is empty the float switch will come to rest
  at the bottom of the tank, causing a switch
  to turn off the pump motor.

- 10 psi low pressure switch located on the motive flow line
- Thermal cut-out switch on the pump. Cold fuel is used to cool
  the pump motor. With the pump on and no fuel left to pump, the
  motor will overheat, causing it to turn off.

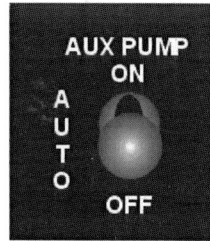

If the auxiliary fuel pump fails, the fuel in the auxiliary tank is
inaccessible. Therefore, standard operation of the auxiliary tanks is to
burn all the fuel in them first in case the auxiliary fuel pump fails. Make
sure the fuel reserve requirements can be met if this occurs. When the
auxiliary pump fails or the tank is empty, a 5 psi low pressure switch
located in the transfer line between the collector and the auxiliary tank
will advise the pilot by illuminating the yellow [L or R NO AUX XFR]
annunciator.

The on position of the auxiliary fuel pump switch can be used when the
auto feature has turned the pump off and there is still fuel in the auxiliary
tank. If one of the auto features has failed but the pump is still operating
normally, this may allow access to the fuel in the auxiliary tank.

Fuel Cross Transfer

The maximum fuel imbalance between tanks is 200 lbs. Fuel from one
wing can supply the opposite engine through a cross transfer system that
transfers fuel from one wing to the other at a rate of 480 pounds of fuel
per hour. The cross transfer valve is located in the left fuel tank, and fuel
can be moved in either direction through the use of the left or right 11 ±

2 standby boost pump. The
cross transfer control switch
is located on the upper fuel
control panel. When the
crossfeed switch is placed
in the left or right position,
one system can supply fuel to the other system. For example, when the
switch is placed in the left position the right standby boost pump
automatically turns on and the cross transfer valve opens, moving fuel

from the right collector tank to the left collector tank. To cross transfer fuel use the following procedure:

1. Standby Pumps - OFF
2. Transfer Flow Switch - LEFT or RIGHT (as required); Check FUEL TRANSFER annunciator - ILLUMINATED
3. Fuel Balance – MONITOR
4. Transfer Flow Switch – OFF (centered) to discontinue fuel transfer.

A white [FUEL TRANSFER] annunciator light illuminates during cross transfer operation. Make sure both standby boost pump switches are in the off position before cross transfer. If the standby boost pump on the receiving side was turned on, both standby boost pumps would oppose each other, not allowing cross transfer to occur. In the event of an inoperative electric boost pump, cross transfer can only be accomplished from the side of the operative pump. If the transfer valve fails, a yellow [XFR VALVE FAIL] annunciator illuminates.

Fuel Vents

There are three fuel vents; a heated ram vent, a flush vent, and a recessed ram vent (see photo to right and fuel system diagram in back of chapter). The heat to the ram vent is controlled by a switch in the cockpit. The design of the recessed ram vent makes it resistant to icing over. The flush vent and heated ram vent provide a slight positive pressure inside the wing. Fuel is first vented from the main tank to the auxiliary tank to relieve overpressure from thermal expansion or when low power settings cause the motive flow line to return fuel and the main tank is already full. If the auxiliary tank is also full, pressure from expanding fuel is automatically vented from the tank through the heated ram vent overboard. There is a flame arrestor on the flush vent and also on the recessed ram vent line to prevent a flame from entering the fuel system from static electricity or a lightning strike.

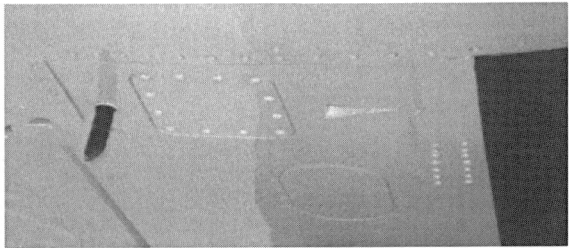

Fuel Drains

To check for fuel contamination, there are 5 drains on the underside of each wing. Normal preflight fuel draining procedures will generally remove most excess water from the fuel tanks. Because jet fuel and water are of similar densities, it takes approximately three hours for any water to settle to the drains after the aircraft is moved or refueled. Water can cause the fuel gauges to read inaccurately. The suspended water will also facilitate the growth of microbiological sludge in settlement areas of the fuel system, which can cause corrosion of metal components and clogging of filters. To help prevent this, most operators use ethylene glycol monomethyl ether (EGME). Better known as "Prist," it absorbs dissolved water in the fuel and lowers the freezing temperature of the fuel.

Fuel Quantity Indicators

The fuel quantity in each wing is measured by capacitance type probes which transmit the pounds of fuel to gauges located on the fuel control panel in the cockpit. The capacitance-type system compensates for changes in fuel temperature and fuel type to provide an accurate indication of fuel quantity

(within 3%).

A two-position switch, placarded FUEL QTY - MAIN/AUX, is located in the lower right side of the fuel control panel. In the main position, the gauges indicate the quantity of fuel in the main and collector tanks in each wing. In the auxiliary position, only the amount of fuel in the auxiliary tank is indicated.

There is also a visual fuel quantity sensor system for use when the normal system is inoperative. There are two sight probes on the underside of each wing. When the probes are submerged in fuel, they are solid black in color, and when not submerged, they are red with a black dot. When the outboard probe is red, it indicates that there is less than 1150 pounds of fuel in that tank. When the inboard probe is red, it indicates that there is less than 745 pounds of fuel in that tank.

RED INDICATES LESS THAN 745 LBS FUEL WITH WINGS LEVEL

NOTE: A quick way to convert jet fuel pounds to gallons is to take the number of pounds of fuel you need, drop the last number (convert 1000 pounds to 100 units) then multiply by 1.5. This is approximately the number of gallons you need.

Use of Aviation Gasoline

Aviation gasoline may be used as an emergency fuel. However, time between engine overhaul will be greatly reduced. Each engine is allowed only 150 hours of operation on aviation gasoline before engine overhaul. If a partial mixture of jet fuel and aviation gasoline is used, the operation time is computed proportional to the mixture. (50% aviation gasoline x 3 hours flight time = 1.5 hours aviation gasoline use) Aviation gas is less dense than jet fuel, therefore operation on aviation gas is prohibited above 18,000 feet or with standby pumps inoperative. Aviation gas feeds well under pressure but cannot suction feed as well. The standby fuel pumps provide an alternate means to pressure feed the system. The standby pumps must also be on for takeoff and landing.

Low Fuel Warning System

There are two low fuel warning annunciators. When there is less than 324 pounds of fuel in the main tanks, a [L or R FUEL QTY] annunciator illuminates. If the fuel in the collector tank drops below 53 pounds, a [L or R COL TANK LOW] annunciator illuminates. The low level sensors are located on the forward side of the tank. Acceleration on takeoff or a climb may result in a low fuel indication prematurely.

Limitations

Approved Engine Fuels

Jet A, Jet A-1, JP-5, JP-8 (JP fuels are military grades)

Jet B, JP-4 (operation is prohibited above 8000 feet if either standby pump is inoperative)

Emergency Engine Fuels

80 Red, 80/87 Red, 91/96, 100 Green, 100/130 Green, 100LL Blue, 115/145 Purple. See section "Use of Aviation Gasoline" for limitations of using these emergency engine fuels.

Fuel Gauges In The Yellow Arc

Do not takeoff if fuel quantity gauges indicate in yellow arc or indicate less than 363 pounds of fuel in each wing system.

Operating With Low Fuel Pressure

Operation of either engine with its corresponding fuel pressure annunciator [L or R FUEL PRES LO] illuminated is limited to 10 hours before overhaul or replacement of the engine driven fuel pump. Windmilling time need not be charged against this time limit.

Fuel System   Beech 1900D

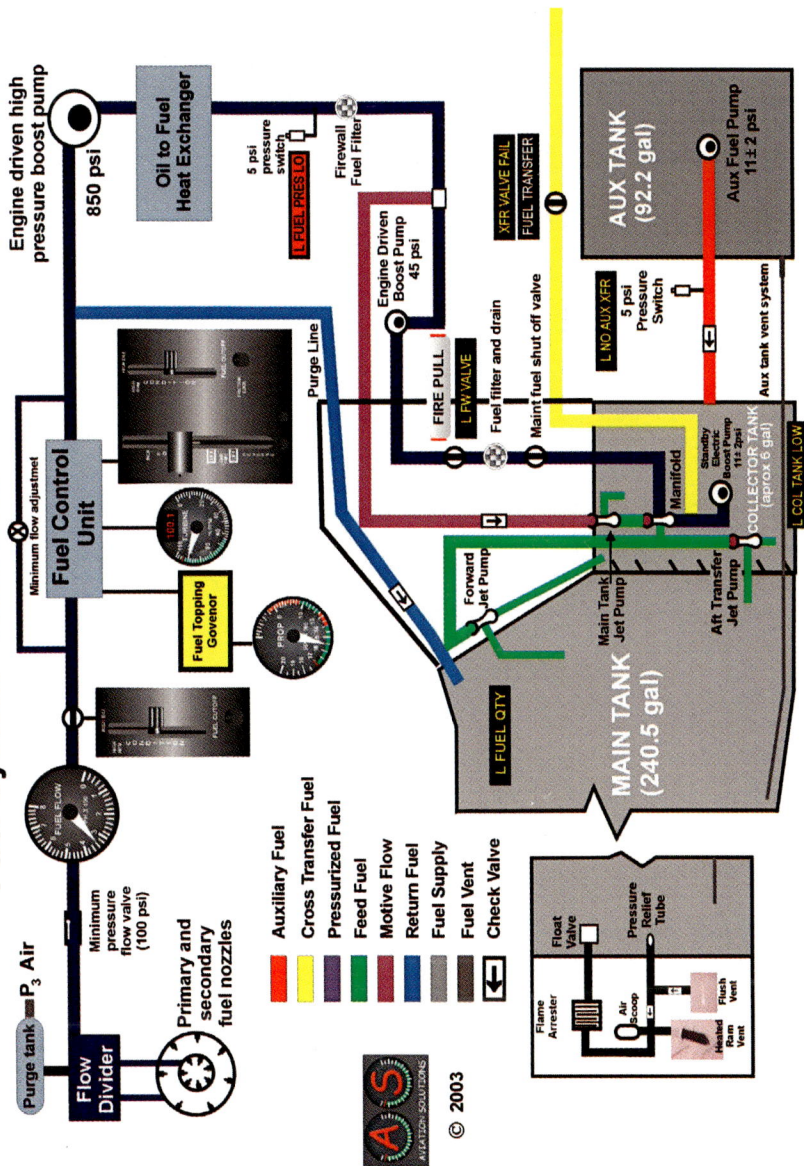

Engine driven high pressure boost pump

850 psi

Oil to Fuel Heat Exchanger

5 psi pressure switch

L FUEL PRES LO

Firewall Fuel Filter

Engine Driven Boost Pump 45 psi

FIRE PULL

L FW VALVE

Fuel filter and drain

Maint fuel shut off valve

Purge Line

Fuel Control Unit

Minimum flow adjustmet

Fuel Topping Govenor

PROP

AUX TANK (92.2 gal)

Aux Fuel Pump 11±2 psi

XFR VALVE FAIL
FUEL TRANSFER

L NO AUX XFR

5 psi Pressure Switch

Aux tank vent system

Manifold

Standby Electric Boost Pump 11±2psi

COLLECTOR TANK (aprox 6 gal)

L COL TANK LOW

Forward Jet Pump

Main Tank Jet Pump

Aft Transfer Jet Pump

MAIN TANK (240.5 gal)

L FUEL QTY

Minimum pressure flow valve (100 psi)

Purge tank — P₃ Air

Flow Divider

Primary and secondary fuel nozzles

- **Auxiliary Fuel**
- **Cross Transfer Fuel**
- **Pressurized Fuel**
- **Feed Fuel**
- **Motive Flow**
- **Return Fuel**
- **Fuel Supply**
- **Fuel Vent**
- **Check Valve**

© 2003

AVIATION SOLUTIONS

Float Valve

Pressure Relief Tube

Flame Arrester

Air Scoop

Flush Vent

Heated Ram Vent

FUEL   **99**

Notes:

Chapter 10
ICE PROTECTION

There are two types of ice protection, anti-ice and de-ice. Anti-icing equipment is designed to prevent the formation of ice and should be used prior to entering icing conditions. The 1900 has heated windshields, fuel vents, a stall warning system, pitot tubes, alternate static ports, an engine air intake lip heat, and an oil-to-fuel heat exchanger. There are also air inlet ice vanes and auto ignition that should be used prior to entering icing conditions.

De-icing equipment removes ice that is already present. For de-icing the 1900 has de-ice boots, propeller heat, and brake heat.

The main panel for ice protection switches (shown below on right) is located on the pilots right subpanel. The remaining ice protection switches are located on the pilots left subpanel (shown below on the left).

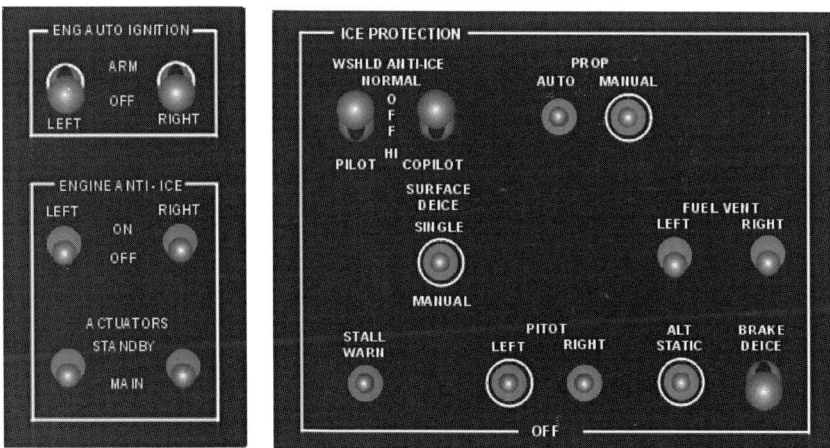

Anti-Ice Systems

Windshield Heat

Both pilot's and copilot's windshields are heated to prevent icing and make them more pliable in case of a bird strike. Windshield heat is designed for continuous in-flight use in any weather condition and should be turned on prior to every takeoff. Windshield heat also aids in preventing frost and fogging due to rapid descents from cooler higher altitudes into warm, moist air. The windshield heat may cause distortion in vision, which is more noticeable at night.

The outer layer of the windshield is coated with a non-electrostatic application (NESA) film to bleed off static electricity. The windshield heat switch can be in one of three positions; normal, high or off. With the switch in the "NORMAL" position, the windshield is heated to a surface temperature to 90°F to 110°F. When the switch is on "HIGH", extra electrical current is used to concentrate the heat (up to the same temperature as in normal mode) to a smaller area (2/3) of the windshield.

The manufacturer recommends a maximum speed of 223 knots in icing conditions to ensure the windshield anti-ice system can heat the windshield sufficiently to melt the accumulating ice. This speed is not a limitation but just a recommendation. If frost or ice begins to accumulate on the windshield with the heat on above this speed (or at any speed), it may be necessary to reduce airspeed to prevent any further accumulation.

NOTE Operation of windshield heat will cause erratic operation of the magnetic compass because it creates a magnetic field around the compass. Windshield heat should be turned off for a period of 15 seconds to allow stabilization of the compass before reading.

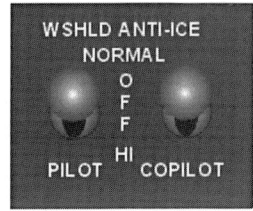

Fuel Vent Heat

Heated ram vents are leather textured, one-inch electrically heated tubes that are located on the underside of each wing by the tip. Fuel vents allow pressure to equalize in the fuel tanks when fuel is used or can also allow excess fuel pressure to vent overboard. The fuel vent heat ensures the vent does not ice over.

Stall Warning Heat

The stall warning transducer vane and plate, located on the leading edge of the left wing, are electrically heated to prevent icing. If stall warning heat is left on during

ICE PROTECTION

ground operations, sensed by left gear safety switch, it will only receive 1/2 of the electrical power, which prevents it from overheating.

In icing conditions, stall speeds increase due to the disruption of airflow over the wing, which causes stall warning devices to lose their accuracy. Any accumulation of ice around the stall warning vane reduces the accuracy in the stall warning system, even if the vane itself is clear of ice. For these reasons, the manufacturer recommends maintaining a minimum speed of 160 knots until a speed decrease is necessary for landing. When slowing for landing, make sure to leave yourself a safe margin over V_{REF} to compensate for inaccuracies in stall warning systems.

If the system fails or is turned off, a yellow [STALL HEAT] annunciator will illuminate.

Pitot Heat

Each pitot tube senses ram air for the airspeed indicator and contains a static port to send data to the static instruments. Each pitot tube can be electrically heated to ensure accurate pitot and static information while in icing conditions. The left pitot tube provides input to the left airspeed and static instruments, and the right pitot tube to the right airspeed and static instruments. During normal operations, the pitot heat is turned on prior to takeoff and left on for the entire flight, regardless of the weather conditions. The pitot heat switches should be off (down) during ground operations, except for testing or for short intervals of time to remove ice or snow from the tube. The left pitot tube heat is powered by two sources in the electrical system for redundancy.

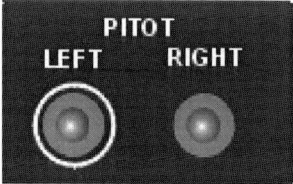

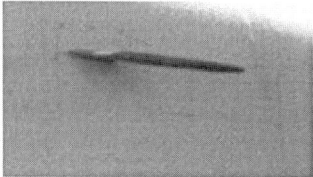

If the system fails or is turned off, a yellow [L or R PITOT HEAT] annunciator will illuminate.

Alternate Static

There are four static ports, two in each pitot tube and one located on each side of the airplane below the cockpit side windows on the lower portion of

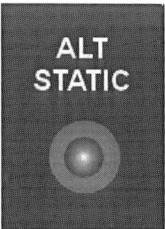

the fuselage. The static ports in the pitot tubes are the primary ones used for normal operations and are heated anytime the pitot heat is on. The static ports on the fuselage are anti-ice by design but they also may be heated to ensure they remain clear of ice. During normal operations, the alternate static heat is turned on prior to takeoff and left on for the entire flight, regardless of the weather conditions.

If the primary static port becomes iced over or plugged, you can select the alternate static source with a switch on the lower cockpit side walls. There are two alternate static sources, one for the pilot side and one for the copilot side instruments. If you use alternate static, the altimeter will read slightly higher and the airspeed slightly faster than actual.

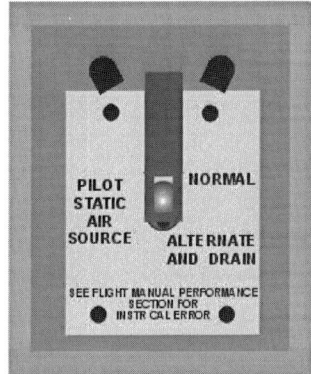

PILOT STATIC AIR SOURCE NORMAL ALTERNATE AND DRAIN
SEE FLIGHT MANUAL PERFORMANCE SECTION FOR INSTR CAL ERROR

Air Inlet Lip Heat

Each engine air inlet lip is continuously heated through the use of exhaust air. Hot air, routed from a scoop in the engine's left side exhaust stack, passes through each air inlet lip and is exhausted through the right side exhaust stack. Since this is done automatically, there is no switch to turn on.

Air Inlet Ice Vanes

Engine ice vanes are a small piece of metal installed in the engine air inlet to help prevent the induction of rain or ice. They also help prevent foreign object damage (FOD) to the compressor turbine by keeping gravel and other loose items from being ingested by the engine. Located just aft of the engine air inlet, air inlet ice vanes deflect rain, ice, and foreign objects down and away from the engine plenum.

Air inlet ice vanes are commonly referred to as inertial separators, boards, torque suppressors, engine anti-ice, vanes, or actuators.

There are four switches on the pilot's left subpanel for the ice vanes. The top two are to extend or retract the left or right ice vane, and the bottom two are used to select which motor is used to power the movement. There are two actuator motors for each ice vane, one main and one standby. The ice vanes can either be extended or retracted and cannot be moved to intermediate positions.

When the top switch is placed to the extend "ON" position, the selected motor lowers the ice vane and opens a bypass door. The ice vane extends into the incoming airflow and, due to the venturi effect, the speed of the air increases and prevents heavier particles (like rain, ice, or gravel) from making the turn at the end of the ice vane and being digested by the engine. Because some of the air exits the engine with the heavier particles through the bypass door, you will experience a slight loss of torque when the ice vanes are extended. This torque can be regained by advancing the power levers, which will increase fuel burn and ITT. Illumination of the green [L or R ENG ANTI-ICE] lights indicates that the vanes are extended.

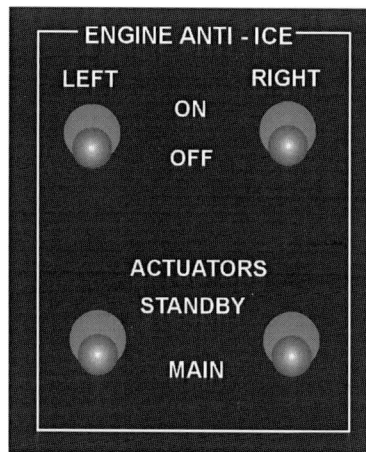

You should extend the ice vanes when in visible moisture (rain, snow, ice, clouds, etc.) at or below +5° Celsius. They also should be extended for all ground operations (provided engine temperature limitations are not exceeded) to prevent FOD to the engine. When flying, the ice vanes should be retracted at +15° Celsius and above to provide sufficient engine oil cooling.

Illumination of a yellow [L or R ENG ICE FAIL] light indicates that the ice vane has not reached its selected position. There are two different conditions that can illuminate the annunciator. First, if the position of the switch does not agree with the micro switch in the ice vane within 30 seconds, it will illuminate. Second, if the motor that you have selected is inoperative, the annunciator will illuminate immediately. If this annunciator is illuminated, the other actuator should be selected.

Oil-to-Fuel Heat Exchangers

Oil-to-fuel heat exchangers are located on the accessory section of the engine. They use engine oil at operating temperature (71°C) to heat the fuel. The fuel lines are placed adjacent to the warm oil lines so there is heat transfer between the two. Heating the fuel prevents thickening in cold temperatures and keeps any water in the fuel from freezing. Under certain flight conditions, the engine oil-to-fuel heater may not be sufficient to prevent ice in the fuel. Using the fuel additive prist lowers the fuel's freezing temperature and can help prevent ice from forming.

Auto Ignition

The ignitors can be used to help prevent an engine flame out caused when ice or water reaches the burner can. When armed, the auto ignition system will turn the ignitors on when engine torque falls below approximately 700 foot pounds and remains on until engine torque accelerates above this threshold.

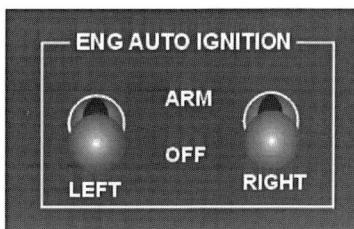

Windshield Wipers

Windshield wipers are installed on both the pilot's and copilot's windshields for snow and rain removal. They are usually only used during taxiing, approach, and landing because once a sufficient amount of airspeed is developed airflow will keep the windshields free of rain or snow. There is one electric motor that runs both wipers. The switch for the wipers is located on the overhead panel. When the switch is held in the spring loaded "PARK" position, the wiper blades are stowed at the center post in a vertical position.

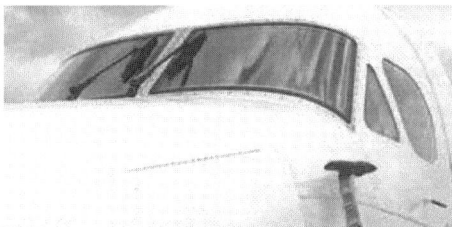

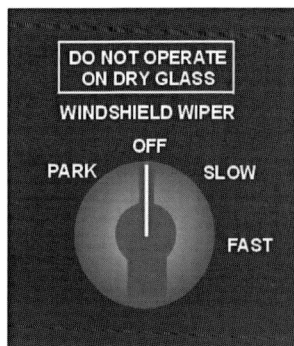

$\begin{smallmatrix} N & O & T_E \\ \end{smallmatrix}$ To protect the NESA coating, do not operate wipers on dry glass.

De-ice Systems

Ice Light

Ice Detection

Wing ice lights,
located on the
outboard side of the
engine nacelles, provide nighttime
illumination of the wings' outboard
leading edges to check for ice
accumulation. The switch for the ice
light (shown to the right) is located on
the overhead panel.

EXTERIOR LIGHTS

ICE

OFF

Surface De-ice

The surface de-ice system removes ice accumulation on the leading
edges of the wings, stabilons, tailets and horizontal stabilizers. De-
ice boots are attached to the leading edges by cement. They are
electrically controlled and use engine bleed air to pneumatically
operated rubber de-ice boots. The de-ice boot is a fabric-reinforced
rubber sheet containing built-in inflation tubes.

To dislodge ice from the leading edges, bleed air is
sent to the boots to make them inflate and crack the
ice. To deflate and hold the boots on the leading
edges, the bleed air passes through an ejector which
creates a vacuum to hold them flat against the
leading edge.

SURFACE
DEICE

SINGLE

MANUAL

The system is controlled by a three-position switch
which is spring-loaded to the center off position.

Actuation of the switch to the "SINGLE" position triggers a system timer which sends bleed air to inflate the outboard wing boots. After approximately six seconds, the timer closes the distributor valve and vacuum is applied to deflate the boots. The timer then opens the distributor valve and sends regulated bleed air to inflate the inboard wing, stabilons, tailets and horizontal stabilizer boots for approximately six seconds. The inflation cycle occurs only once each time the switch is activated. Selecting the "MANUAL" position bypasses the timer, and all the boots will inflate and remain inflated until the switch is released and returns to the center off position. The switch should be held in the manual position until the three green advisory lights [INBD WG DEICE], [OUTBD WG DEICE], [TAIL DEICE] illuminate, indicating when the outboard, inboard, and tail boots are inflated. The manual system uses a lot off bleed air since inflates all the boots and the same time. The pneumatic pressure may drop low enough to momentarily illuminate the warning [L and R BLEED AIR FAIL] annunciators.

A pneumatic pressure gauge should fluctuate each time bleed air is sent to the wings, and the gyro suction gauge should fluctuate each time bleed air is used to create the vacuum to deflate the boots. The gauges are located in the copilot's right subpanel.

For the de-ice boots to properly crack and remove ice, an accumulation of at least 1 to 1 1/2 inches of ice must be present. If the boots are inflated too soon, the ice may not crack and will expand with the boot (called bridging). This leaves a gap between the leading edge and the ice which will cause any additional attempts at breaking the ice to fail.

To properly judge the amount of ice build-up on the wings, look at the end of the wing where there is a diffuser for the strobe lights. There is a hole that sits 2 inches from the leading edge to look through to see if the position lights are working. When ice begins to block the hole, it's time to pop the boots.

Be wary of captains who pop boots prior to a copilot greasing on a landing. This disrupts the airflow over the wing at slow speeds making a greaser turn into a hard landing.

Permanent damage to the de-ice boots can occur if they are operated in temperatures below -40° F.

Propeller De-ice

Propeller de-ice boots, bonded to the leading edges of the propeller blades, are designed to electrically heat the boot to melt ice and allow the centrifugal force of the heated water to melt ice on the remainder of the blade. It is normally used as anti-ice and turned on prior to entering icing conditions.

Each de-ice boot has one heater. Automatic de-icing is accomplished by heating all the elements on the right and then the left propeller, for 90 seconds each, in a sequence controlled by a timer. In the automatic mode the loadmeter should increase .05%.

As a backup to the automatic de-ice system, a manual system is installed. Manual de-icing is accomplished by holding the switch to the "MANUAL" position for approximately 90 seconds until the ice is dislodged. This switch overrides the system timer and heats all the elements on both propellers simultaneously. Proper operation of the manual system is indicated by an increase of approximately .10% on the loadmeters. When the red [L or R OIL PRES LO] annunciator illuminates in aircraft with serial number UE 262 and after the auto mode of propeller de-ice deactivates and only the manual mode will be operative.

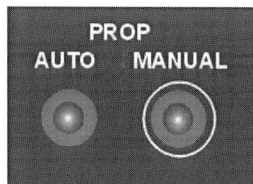

If the de-ice boot does not remove ice evenly, a propeller imbalance may occur. This imbalance can be relieved by varying the prop RPM; increase RPM briefly and return to desired setting, repeating if necessary.

NOTE To prevent system damage, operate the propeller de-ice system only when the engines are running.

With the propeller de-icing system "ON", the prop de-ice ammeter needle should be within the green arc (32-38 amps) for normal operation. If the ammeter reads 0 amps when the system is turned on, the prop de-ice is inoperative and cannot be used. An ammeter reading less than 32 amperes indicates that one or more of the boots is not functioning properly. If propeller de-ice is used under this condition, you can expect an uneven build up of ice which causes undesirable vibration.

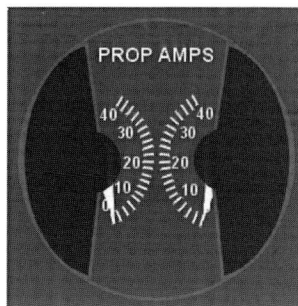

NOTE

While the heated water is dislodging ice from the remainder of the propeller blade, ice chunks may hit the fuselage, causing passenger alarm. Inform passengers of this possibility when in icing conditions.

Brake De-ice

Brake de-ice is installed on the main wheels to prevent ice and slush from building up between the wheels and freezing the brakes. Unregulated bleed air from the engine P_3 valve is used to provide brake de-icing. Placing the switch in the on (up) position directs the bleed air to the brake assembly. If the switch is left on after take-off and gear retraction, the gear uplock switch activates a timer, which will close the solenoid valve after 8 to 12 minutes, preventing heat damage to landing gear. To reactivate brake de-ice after it automatically turns off, extend the landing gear and cycle the brake de-ice switch to off and then to on. A green [L or R BK DEICE ON] annunciator light illuminates when the system is on.

The bleed air lines to the brakes are enclosed in a low pressure (18 psi) tubing called ethylene vinyl acetate. If the bleed air line ruptures, the hot bleed air (400° F) will melt the outer tubing, causing the pressure to drop below 1.5 psi. This will cause a [L or R BK DI OVHT] annunciator to illuminate. When a brake de-ice overheat annunciator is illuminated, you must turn off the brake de-ice system.

Radar

Weather radar is installed and is displayed on the EHSI EFIS display located just below the attitude indicator. It will display the current heading and 30° each direction of center.

The control panel for the radar is located on the pedestal. The range can be adjusted from 10 miles out to 300 miles, although with the 12 inch antenna installed in the nose cone, it can not detect much precipitation beyond 150 miles. The gain is used to adjust the sensitivity of how much precipitation is needed to display a return on the EHSI. The tilt is used to move the radar antenna up and down to help you determine how high a storm is.

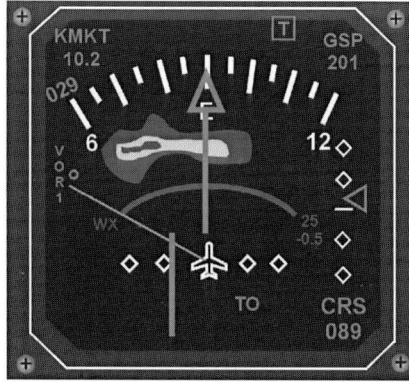

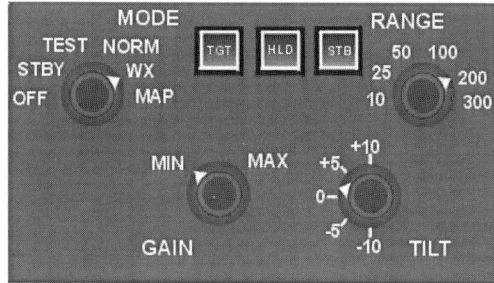

Notes:

Chapter 11

AVIONICS

Avionics installed in the 1900D include the Communication and Navigation Radios, EFIS system, TCAS, GPWS, radar, cabin briefer, and cockpit voice recorder. All of the items are powered "on" with the avionics master switch located on the pilots lower left subpanel. Because of the high electrical draw of the avionics equipment and the surge of electrical power through the system during an engine start, the avionics master switch is normally left off until the generators are online after the engines are started. If the avionics need to be powered on the ground without a generator online, use a ground power unit (GPU) to conserve battery power.

The avionics master switch makes it convenient to turn all these items off with one switch. If the switch fails, power can be supplied to the avionics equipment by pulling the 5 amp "AVIONICS MASTER" circuit breaker in the upper right corner of the circuit breaker panel. It takes electrical power through the avionics master switch to turn the equipment off.

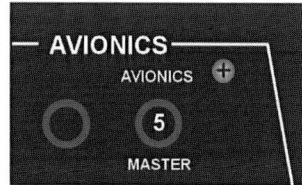

Audio Panel

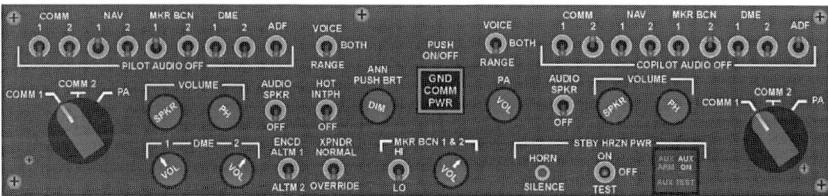

The audio panel is in the center of the instrument panel. The left side controls the pilot side audio and the right side controls the copilot audio.

Audio Source

Along the top of the panel, there are 9 switches on both the pilot side and copilot side that control which audio source comes through the headsets or cockpit speaker. Placing a switch in the up position turns that audio source on. Audio sources that are selected on always come through the headset as long as a headset is

plugged into the jack. To get audio to come over the pilot or copilot cockpit speaker, the appropriate "AUDIO SPKR" switch needs to be turned on. With the cockpit speaker off, all audio, with the exception of aural warning tones, is inhibited. On 1900D models with serial number UE-262 and after, all cockpit audio, including aural warning tones, are inhibited from the speaker with the speaker switch off.

Transmit Selector

The large rotary knobs on the lower left and right of the audio panel control what the pilot or copilot transmit on when pressing the push to talk switch (COMM 1, 2, or PA). When selecting COMM 1 or 2 to transmit, the corresponding receiver is automatically selected on.

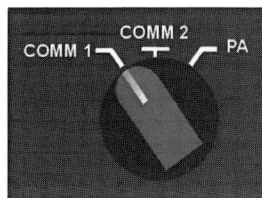

Volume Knobs

There are a total of 8 volume knobs; one for the cockpit speaker and headphones for both the pilot and copilot, two for DME identification, one for marker beacon identification, and one for the PA volume in the cabin.

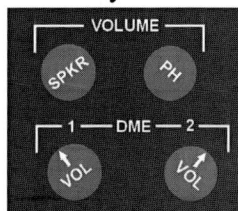

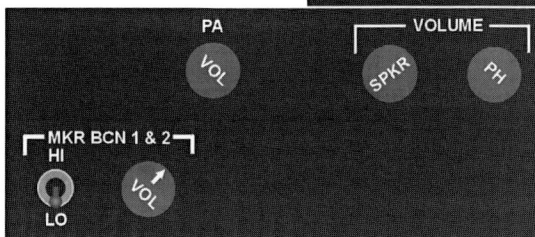

Nav Ident

The VOICE/BOTH/RANGE switch controls which portion of the NAV or ADF identification you hear when the ADF or NAV 1 or 2 audio source is selected on. In the VOICE position, the voice portion of the audio is heard but not the Morse code identification. In the RANGE position, only the Morse code identification is heard. In the BOTH position, the voice and range are heard.

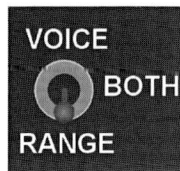

Hot Interphone

The hot interphone switch is below the pilot side VOICE/BOTH/RANGE switch. This switch is normally left on and allows for direct communication between crewmembers when headsets are on. With

the switch off, each pilot must press the interphone switch on the left side of the yoke to break the squelch to communicate through the headsets.

Encoding Altimeter Selector

The encoding altimeter selector switch (ENCD ALTM 1/ALTM 2) controls whether the pilot (ALTM 1) or copilot (ALTM 2) encoding altimeter sends altitude information to the TCAS, GPWS, and GPS.

Ground Comm Power

The GND COMM PWR button is in the center of the audio panel. Normally, the battery and avionics master switch needs to be on to turn on the com radios. To conserve battery power if you just need to pick up ATIS or a clearance, you can push the GND COMM PWR button, to turn on COMM 1 when the battery switch is off.

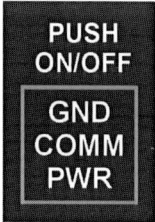

Marker Beacon

The volume and sensitivity switch for the marker beacons is below the GND COMM PWR button. The switch and dial control both the pilot and copilot audio simultaneously.

Standby Horizon Power

A standby horizon power system is installed as a backup to the pilot's EADI. The auxiliary battery, located in the nose avionics compartment, is powerful enough to operate standby horizon for a minimum of 30 minutes.

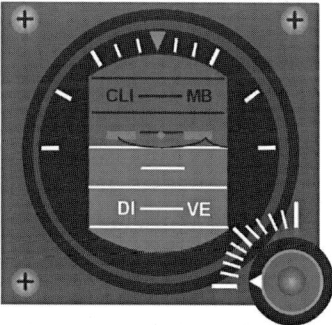

The control panel for the auxiliary power is on the audio panel. With the standby horizon power switch on, the avionics master switch on, and the standby horizon being

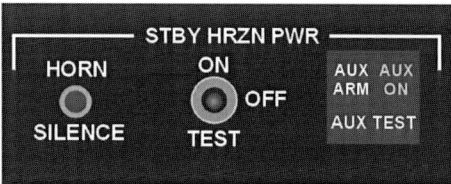

powered by the right generator bus the green AUX ARM annunciator illuminates. If voltage to the standby horizon drops below 18 volts, the yellow AUX ON annunciator illuminates along with a steady warning horn. You can silence the horn by pressing the horn silence button next to the standby horizon power switch. The horn will sound, and the AUX ON annunciator will illuminate during shutdown if the avionics master switch is turned off before the standby horizon power switch is turned off.

To test the auxiliary battery hold the standby horizon power switch to the test position until the AUX TEST annunciator illuminates. If the AUX TEST annunciator does not illuminate, even momentarily, within 5 seconds of holding the switch to the test position, consult with maintenance.

With the standby horizon power switch on, the auxiliary battery is not connected to the standby gyro until the left squat switch senses the aircraft in the air. This prevents the auxiliary battery from powering the standby gyro while on the ground. The auxiliary battery is continuously charged by the right generator bus.

Dim Function

The ANN PUSH BRT rotary push button dial dims the lights on the avionics for nighttime operations. When the knob is pulled out, the lights dim. Turning the dial changes the intensity of the avionics lights.

Transponder Override

The transponder is wired through the ground squat switch, so even if the transponder is turned on it will not operate while on the ground. The transponder can operate on the ground when the XPNDR NORMAL/OVERRIDE switch is in the OVERRIDE position.

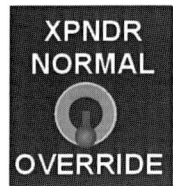

TCAS

Traffic Collision Avoidance System (TCAS) is an optional piece of avionics equipment that has been developed to enhance the safety of flight. TCAS scans the area around the aircraft for other transponder equipped aircraft and displays the traffic on a dedicated display in the cockpit.

When TCAS is installed, it is usually the BFGoodrich model TCAS791. This model is TCAS I system. Current technology in TCAS has led to the development of TCAS II. That technology has not become cost effective enough for many regional, business, and general aviation aircraft. The biggest difference between the systems is the TCAS I does not require a mode S transponder and does not issue resolution advisories (i.e. climb, descend, or monitor vertical speed) after traffic alerts. The TCAS can only track other aircraft that have an operating transponder.

Following is a general review of the technology for information only. Refer to the AFM and BFGoodrich's Pilot Guide for the TCAS for specific and more detailed information. Access BFGoodrich's web site (www.goodrich.com) to download the Pilots Guide for the TCAS.

The TCAS791 display is located in the lower middle portion of the instrument panel and can track up to 35 aircraft at once, with a maximum of 8 being displayed. It will display the 8 targets that are most threatening. The TCAS can detect traffic within 35 miles and +/- 10,000 feet of your aircrafts current altitude.

To turn the TCAS on, turn the DIM/OFF button clockwise to an intensity that you can see the display. The system turns on into standby mode. Pressing the RNG button turns the unit on to start displaying traffic. The TCAS system automatically switches to standby mode 24 seconds after landing detected by the left main gear squat switch.

TA Alert

The traffic is displayed as one of four symbols. An aircraft target that is displayed as a round yellow circle is considered a traffic advisory (TA). A TA is issued along with an audio "Traffic, Traffic" alert. If the other aircraft has a mode C transponder, their altitude is displayed relative (+ or − in hundreds of feet; i.e +02 means the other aircraft is detected 200 feet above your altitude) to your aircraft's altitude. If the aircraft is climbing or descending greater than 500

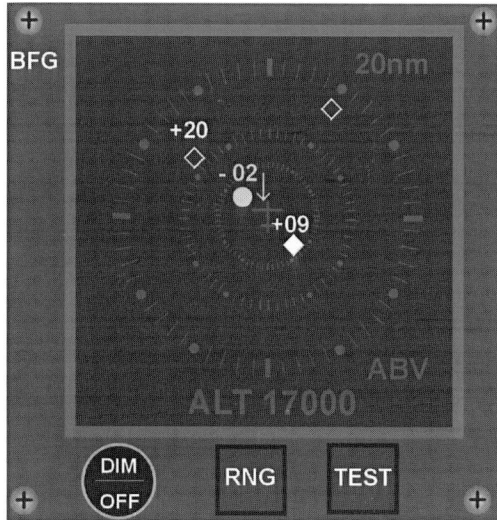

feet/minute, an arrow displays to the right of the target display to indicate the climb or descent.

When traffic is considered a TA depends on aircraft altitude. When the radio altimeter senses the aircraft below 2000 feet AGL, a TA displays when an aircraft is within 15 (non altitude reporting traffic) to 20 (with altitude reporting) seconds of a possible collision or within .2 NM and +/- 600 feet. When above 2000 feet AGL, the parameters increase to within 20 to 30 seconds or .55 NM and +/- 800 feet. The target remains a yellow circle for a minimum of 8 seconds or as long as it is inside the parameters listed above. The audio "Traffic, Traffic" alert mutes when below 400 feet AGL to minimize distraction to the pilots during takeoff and landing. In UE-262 and after, this and all other audio alerts are only heard through the headsets unless the AUDIO SPKR switch is on.

If a TA is detected but the aircraft is outside the range selected on the display, a yellow semi-circle shows at the edge of the display according to the aircrafts bearing with the altitude readout (if available).

If a bearing is not detected by the omni directional antenna for another aircraft but meets the TA criteria, a "TA 1.0 +05" annunciator illuminates below the aircraft symbol. The digits after the TA are the distance and relative altitude (if altitude reporting) to your aircraft.

PA Alert and Other Traffic Symbol

An aircraft target that is not a TA but within 4 NM and +/- 1200 feet displays as a solid white diamond and is called a proximity advisory (PA). Non-altitude reporting traffic is considered to be at your altitude. An open white triangle is used to display all other traffic targets.

Altitude Range

The TCAS unit can display three different altitude ranges. In the normal mode, aircraft within +/- 2700 feet of your current aircraft altitude are displayed. In the Look Up (above) mode, aircraft detected from 2700 feet below to 9000 feet above your aircraft altitude are displayed. Similarly in the Look Down below mode, aircraft detected from 2700 feet above to 9000 feet below you aircraft are displayed. To select different the modes, press the TEST button (while in the air or on the ground with the TCAS not in standby) below the TCAS display to rotate through the different

(NRM, ABV, and BLW) modes. The current mode is annunciated in the lower right of the TCAS display.

At the bottom of the display, your aircraft's current altitude is annunciated. If the altitude displayed is not within +/- 250 feet of the altitude on your barometric altimeter, consult maintenance.

Distance Range

In the air, the TCAS can display a ring of up to 20 nautical miles around the aircraft to display traffic. There are three settings for the range of the display while in the air; 5, 10, or 20 nm. Pressing the RNG button on the bottom of the display rotates through the available ranges. The range selected is annunciated in the upper right corner of the display. In the 5 nm range, the inner ring represents 2 nm with the outer ring 5 nm. In the 10 and 20 nm ranges there are three rings; inner, middle, and outer. In the 10 nm range; the rings represent 2, 5, and 10 nm. In the 20 nm range; the rings represent 5, 10, and 20 nm. On the ground, only the 5 and 10 nm ranges may be selected. Also only while on the ground, pressing the RNG button while the TCAS is in the standby mode turns the TCAS on in the 10 nm range with the ABV display.

TCAS Test

The TCAS system can be tested while on the ground and in the standby mode. Pressing the test button initiates the units self test. A successful test is annunciated by a test screen similar to the one shown to the right and an audio "TCAS test passed". If the self test detects a problem, the display has large text across the center of the screen "TCAS FAILED" with an audio alert "TCAS test failed".

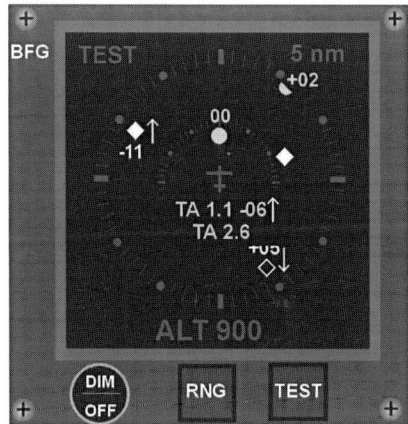

GPWS

GPWS was designed to reduce the accident rate associated with Controlled Flight Into Terrain (CFIT). It provides audio and visual alerts to the crew when the airplane penetrates a predetermined envelope above the terrain.

Ground Proximity Warning System (GPWS) is a brand of Terrain Awareness and Warning System (TAWS) that is designed to help prevent Controlled Flight Into Terrain (CFIT) accidents. Having GPWS installed is estimated to decrease the chances of being involved in a CFIT accident by one third. The GPWS takes inputs from the radio altimeter, copilots pitot static system, glideslope, flap handle, autopilot, and landing gear and applies alerting algorithms to alert the flight crew through annunciators and aural alerts when the preset parameters are exceeded.

There are two types of TAWS that are typically installed in the 1900D. The Honeywell Mark VI GPWS or a Honeywell EGPWS. Following is a general review of the technology for information only. Refer to the supplement section of the AFM and Honeywell's Pilot Guide for the model of GPWS and EGPWS installed for specific and more detailed information. Pilot guides for the different model GPWS' can be ordered at www.honeywell.com.

Mark VI GPWS

The GPWS has 6 modes of operation:

Mode 1

When the GPWS senses an excessive descent rate in relation to the aircraft's height above the ground, an aural "SINK RATE" alert sounds. If the aircraft continues the excessive descent rate, the aural "SINK RATE" alert sounds again and could be followed by a "PULL UP" alert repeated continuously as the aircraft enters the warning envelope. Sink rate is monitored when below 2500 feet AGL. The specific descent rate that sets the GPWS off gets more sensitive the as the aircraft approaches the ground.

Mode 2

When the terrain rises rapidly underneath the aircraft, like when flying low over a ridge, the GPWS sounds an aural "TERRAIN, TERRAIN" alert. The "TERRAIN, TERRAIN" call is followed by "PULL UP" sounding continuously if the closure rate increases into the warning envelope. The GPWS monitors the closure rate of the radio altimeter when below 2000 feet AGL. For climb out, cruise, and initial approach (flaps not in landing position) the larger alert and warning envelope provides for additional protection. With flaps in the landing position and for the first 60 seconds after departure, the envelope is desensitized to reduce nuisance alerts.

Mode 3

If the aircraft descends after takeoff or a missed approach, the GPWS sounds an aural "DON'T SINK" command every 3 seconds. The aural alert also sounds anytime you begin a go around after descending below 170 feet AGL and the gear or flaps are not in the landing configuration. The amount of altitude loss that triggers the alert depends on the aircraft's height above ground. The alert does not sound above 925 feet AGL.

Mode 4

Mode 4a is active in cruise flight with the gear up. If the gear is not down and locked and the aircraft descends below 500 feet AGL with airspeed below 178 knots, a "TOO LOW GEAR" warning sounds. This mode also protects the aircraft from flying into terrain when the aircraft is not descending excessively (mode 1) or terrain is not raising rapidly (mode 2). When below 750 feet AGL and above 178 knots with the gear up, the GPWS sounds an aural "TOO LOW TERRAIN" warning.

Mode 4b is active in cruise and approach with the gear down and flaps not in the landing configuration. Below 170 feet AGL and less than 150 knots with the gear down and the flaps up, the GPWS sounds an aural "TOO LOW FLAPS" warning. If the flaps are inoperative, there is a "GPWS FLAP OVRD" push button that resets the parameters of the GPWS (modes 1, 2, 3, and 4) to the flaps down settings even if the flaps are up. When the switch is pressed, the background of the annunciator illuminates blue. Mode 4b also protects for terrain clearance like mode 4a does. If above 150 knots up to a maximum of 750 feet AGL with the gear down and flaps not in the landing configuration, an aural "TOO LOW TERRAIN" warning sounds when the aircraft is flown into the protection envelope.

Mode 4c is for protection during takeoff or missed approach with the gear and flaps up while below 2400 feet AGL when the closure rate is less than the mode 2 alert. This mode takes into account an averaged radio altitude to determine a minimum terrain clearance altitude that will sound an aural "TOO LOW TERRAIN" warning if the aircraft is flown into this envelope.

Mode 5

The below glideslope mode of the GPWS becomes active if an ILS frequency is being received on NAV 1, the localizer is within 2 dots of center, the gear is down, and the airplane is below 1000 feet AGL. With the glideslope mode active and when the aircraft is flown 1.3 dots or more below the glideslope, the GPWS sounds an aural "GLIDESLOPE" warning. If the aircraft is flown more than 2 dots below glideslope when below 300 feet AGL, the alert gets louder. When an aural glideslope alert is issued, the "BELOW G/S P/CANCEL" annunciator illuminates. If pressed, either prior to descending below the glideslope or after the GPWS has issued the alert, the aural alerts are cancelled. The press to cancel button only functions when the pilot's glideslope is not flagged, the gear is down, and the aircraft is below 2000 feet AGL. When the mode is cancelled, a "G/S CANCLD" annunciator illuminates below the pilot side VSI on the instrument panel.

Once the switch is pressed, you cannot reset it by pressing the switch again. The system resets itself automatically when any of the following occur:

- The aircraft descends below 30 feet AGL.
- The #1 Nav is changed to a VOR frequency then cycled back to receive an ILS frequency.
- The aircraft climbs above 2000 feet AGL.

Mode 6

The GPWS makes advisory callouts to provide additional situational awareness for the pilots. When the radio altimeter senses the aircraft 500 feet AGL, the GPWS announces a "FIVE HUNDRED" aural call out. When a decision height is set into the EADI and the radio altimeter senses the aircraft has reached that altitude, the GPWS announces a "MINIMUMS, MINIMUMS" aural callout.

An optional feature of mode 6 is a bank angle monitor. Above 210 feet AGL, if bank angle exceeds 50° the GPWS sounds an aural "BANK ANGLE, BANK ANGLE" alert. From 10 feet AGL to 210 feet AGL the bank angle that sets the aural alert off varies between 15° and 50°. If the autopilot is on, the 210 feet AGL upper bank angle call out limit is lowered to 156 feet AGL.

Pilot Action

GPWS alerts that include a "PULL UP" command require the pilot to immediately and positively pull up, set power to maximum rated thrust, and climb at the best angle of climb until the warning ceases.

All other GPWS aural alerts recommend the pilot to initiate corrective action to remove the cause of the warning.

Preflight Test

To test the GPWS, press and hold the "GPWS P/TEST" button on the instrument panel. A successful test is indicated by hearing the aural alerts "GLIDESLOPE, PULL UP, PULL UP, PULL UP".

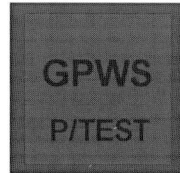

GPWS
P/TEST

Failures

If there is a fault sensed in the GPWS system a "GPWS INOP" annunciator illuminates on the instrument panel.

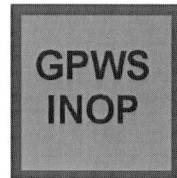

GPWS
INOP

EGPWS

The Enhanced Ground Proximity Warning System (EGPWS) is the more technologically advanced model of TAWS over the GPWS. The major enhancement is the ability to use an internal GPS to compare the aircraft position to an internal terrain database that provides for more accurate and timely alerts. Having the EGPWS is estimated to decrease the chance of having a CFIT accident to one in 30 million (10 times less than with a GPWS). The EGPWS has all the features of the GPWS plus the following additional features.

- Internal GPS with terrain database
- Warning mode enhancements
- Terrain mapping
- Windshear detection

Internal GPS with Terrain Database

Having the internal GPS and terrain database has reduced the amount of non genuine GPWS alerts and increased the lead time some warnings are issued. Knowing the aircrafts present position, altitude, and ground speed; and comparing that to a digitized topographical map allows for a more accurate interpretation of a potential CFIT situation.

The EGPWS terrain database contains the following data:

- Obstacles over 100 feet AGL within the terrain database coverage area.
- Airport runway data for all runways over 2000 feet.
- Terrain data of different degrees of resolution.

There are two modes of the EGPWS associated with the terrain database. Mode TA is terrain and obstacle awareness and mode TCF is the terrain clearance floor.

Terrain and Obstacle Awareness

The TA mode monitors the aircrafts terrain and obstacle clearance and looks ahead of the aircraft for potential conflicts. Beginning at ¼ mile and extending out 3 degrees laterally the TA mode projects down, forward, then up from the aircraft to scan for conflicts. The first alert issued if the aircraft is flown into the safety envelope (typically 40 to 60 seconds ahead of the conflict) is an aural "CAUTION TERRAIN" or "CAUTION OBSTACLE" alert along with a yellow [GPWS] annunciator. If the aircraft continues to fly closer to the terrain or obstacle (typically 30 seconds ahead of the conflict) the aural alert changes to "TERRAIN, TERRAIN, PULL UP, PULL UP" or "OBSTACLE, OBSTACLE, PULL UP, PULL UP" and a red [PULL-UP] annunciator illuminates.

Terrain Clearance Floor

The TCF mode creates a terrain clearance floor around an airport. It alerts the pilots of a descent below the floor regardless of the aircraft configuration. The floor is determined based on current aircraft location, nearest runway, and AGL altitude. If the aircraft is flown below the TCF an aural "TOO LOW TERRAIN" alert sounds along with the yellow [GPWS] annunciator. If the aircraft continues into the TCF, the aural alert changes to "TERRAIN, TERRAIN, PULL-UP" with the red [PULL-UP] annunciator.

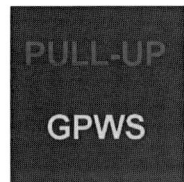

Runway Field Clearance Floor

A Runway Field Clearance Floor (RFCF) has been incorporated into the EGPWS to improve terrain clearance protection around airports like Telluride, CO, where the runway is significantly higher than the surrounding terrain (up on a plateau). Based on aircraft position and height above the airports runway, the RFCF issues an aural "TOO LOW TERRAIN" alert when descending below a normal approach altitude even though the aircraft is sufficiently above the terrain right below the aircraft.

Runway Database

As an aircraft with the gear and flaps down approaches a runway in the airport's database the EGPWS thinks you are landing and increases the parameters to reduce non genuine alerts. Most CFIT accidents occur near an airport, so the degree of resolution for terrain is enhanced in the airport area.

If an airport is not in the EGPWS database, the system thinks the aircraft is descending into a CFIT scenario, which creates numerous aural and visual alerts even though the aircraft may be safely descending for landing. Pressing the [TERR INHIBIT] button suppresses the EGPWS terrain alerts. Push the [TERR INHIBIT] button within 15 miles of the arrival airport that is not in the system's database or if the GPS is degraded or inoperative. Pushing the [TERR INHIBIT] button does not affect the basic GPWS modes 1-6.

If the enhanced terrain features of the EGPWS fails, [TERR INOP] illuminates on the instrument panel.

Terrain Alerting and Display

An optional feature of the EGPWS is the Terrain Alerting and Display (TAD) which is a graphic display of the surrounding terrain on the EHSI screen. It displays terrain that is either above or up to 2000 feet below the aircraft according to the following table:

Terrain/Obstacle Location	Display
Sets off a "PULL UP" warning	Solid Red
Sets off a caution alert	Solid Yellow
2000 feet above aircraft	50% red fill
1000 to 2000 feet above aircraft	50% yellow fill
500 feet below to 1000 feet above aircraft	25% yellow fill
500 to 1000 feet below aircraft	50% green fill
1000 to 2000 feet below aircraft	16% green fill
More than 2000 feet below aircraft or within 400 feet of nearest runway elevation	No display

The TAD feature cannot be on at the same time the weather radar is on. The TAD also has a pop up display that works whenever there is a terrain alert from the EGPWS. When the terrain alert occurs, the terrain display automatically shows on the EHSI, overriding the weather radar display. The TAD feature is meant for situational awareness only and not to be used for navigational purposes. Not all the NOAA terrain data the EGPWS uses as a database is completely accurate.

A software upgrade to the optional TAD display is a feature that displays terrain peaks. This feature is independent of aircraft altitude and displays the digital elevation height of the highest and lowest displayed terrain. The peaks of high relative altitude display as shades of green even if they are more than 2000 feet below the aircraft. It also represents sea level water in blue.

Geometric altitude

Geometric altitude is a GPS-derived altitude designed to eliminate or reduce altimetry errors from temperature extremes, non standard pressures, and crew not setting the altimeter correctly. Having the EGPWS use the geometric altitude enhances the terrain display and alerts.

Windshear

Mode 7, an optional addition to the enhanced feature of the EGPWS, is a windshear function. The windshear mode becomes active below 1500 feet AGL during takeoff and approach. There is a caution and warning feature, both with visual and aural annunciators.

When the EGPWS senses a decreasing headwind, increasing tailwind, or severe vertical downdrafts an aural "WINDSHEAR, WINDSHEAR, WINDSHEAR" alert sounds and a red [W/S WARN] annunciator illuminates.

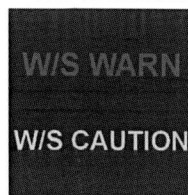

When the EGPWS senses an increasing headwind, decreasing tailwind, or severe vertical updrafts an aural "CAUTION WINDSHEAR" alert sounds and a yellow [W/S CAUTION] annunciator illuminates.

If a failure occurs in the windshear detection function, a "WSHR INOP" annunciator illuminates on the instrument panel.

Preflight Test

Pressing the GPWS P/TEST button initiates a self test of the EGPWS. When the button is pressed, the system checks for any configuration errors. If an error is detected, an aural annunciation of the error sounds (i.e. TERRAIN INOP). If no configuration errors are detected, the system continues the self test with the following indications (may differ due to optional features installed, see AFM for appropriate test procedures for aircraft specific installations):

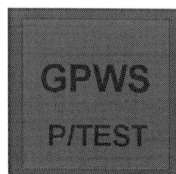

- GPWS INOP and TERR INOP annunciators illuminate.
- GPWS FLAP OVRD annunciator momentarily illuminates.
- BELOW G/S annunciator momentarily illuminates while aural GLIDESLOPE announced over speaker or headset.
- G/S CANCEL annunciator momentarily illuminates.
- PULL UP annunciator momentarily illuminates while aural PULL UP and TERRAIN, TERRAIN, PULL UP announced over speaker or headset.
- Terrain test pattern is displayed on EHSI.
- GPWS INOP and TERR INOP annunciators extinguish.

- Any inoperative features detected issues an aural annunciation (i.e. GLIDESLOPE INOP).

Cabin Briefer

The cabin briefer allows for the crew, at the press of a button, to play a prerecorded briefing for the passengers allowing the crew to focus their attention on other tasks. Think of it as an autopilot for passenger briefings. Turning the rotary dial on the left to the appropriate mode and pressing the green button on the right side of the panel starts the briefing. Pressing the green button again stops the briefing.

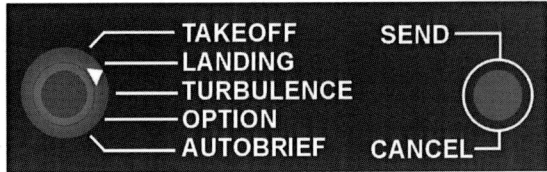

Chapter 12

ELECTRONIC FLIGHT INSTRUMENTATION SYSTEM (EFIS)

The 1900D incorporates a 4 tube EFIS display. The traditional attitude indicator and HSI on both the pilot and copilot side has been replaced with 4 inch by 4 inch EADI and EHSI color CRT displays. The advantage of the EFIS display is additional information, such as weather radar, decision height, waypoints, and status messages, can be displayed with attitude and navigation information. The system incorporates all the information in a central scan and allows the pilot to select or deselect information depending on the segment of flight (i.e. enroute or approach).

The EFIS power control panel is located on the pedestal. Four switches turn on the pilot and copilot side EADI, EHSI, display select panel (DSP), and display processor units (DPU). The switches shown to the right 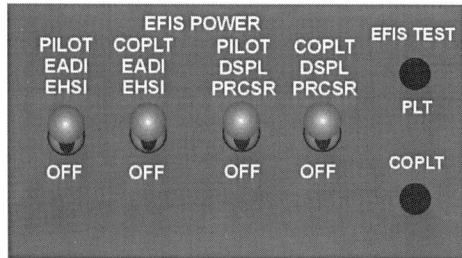 are the modified version of the EFIS power control panel. Aircraft not updated with the kit have push button power switches instead of the lever locked toggle switches.

EADI

The Electronic Attitude Director Indicator (EADI) incorporates familiar attitude information with both lateral and vertical flight path deviation information. In addition, the display also includes the following features: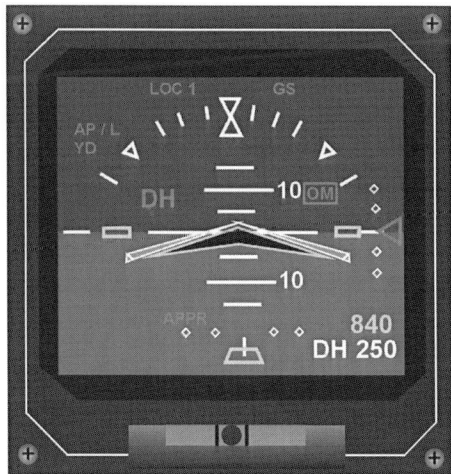

- Aircraft Symbol and Command Bar
- Glide Slope Information
- Lateral Deviation Information

- Inclinometer
- Radio Altimeter
- Decision Height Annunciation
- Marker Beacon Display
- Flight Control Mode Annunciation
- Autopilot/Yaw Damper Engage Status
- Vertical Sync Status
- Trim Status
- Comparator Warnings
- Warning Annunciators

Aircraft Symbol and Command Bar

The aircraft symbol is a stationary representation of the aircraft. The display behind the symbol moves to show pitch and roll.

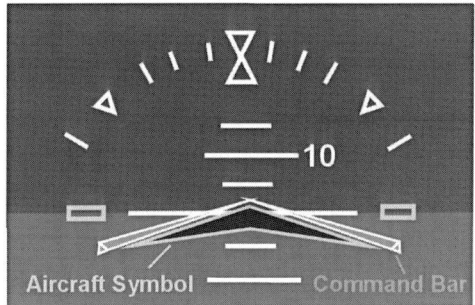

When the flight director is being used, command bars display vertical and roll commands to direct the flight path to what mode the flight director has been selected to control (i.e. altitude hold, nav, or maintain a glide slope). The command bars will move up and down to command a climb or descent, and turn left or right to command a bank to maintain the desired flight path. Flying the aircraft symbol directly below the command bars and keeping it there ensures the selected flight path is maintained.

Glide Slope Information

Like an HSI, the right side of the EADI has a glide slope display. Each triangle represents ½ degree deviation. When a localizer back course is sensed, the glide slope scale is removed from the display, and a "B/C" annunciator illuminates in its place.

Lateral Deviation Information

A scale and box along the bottom of the EADI displays deviations from a selected lateral navigation path. There are two diamonds on

---

either side of a vertical line center index. The yellow lateral deviation box can display a VOR, Localizer, Loran, or GPS course.

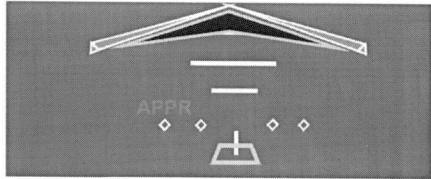

Inclinometer

There is not a turn and bank indicator in the 1900D. To indicate a coordinated turn, an inclinometer is installed on the lower front of the EADI. The inclinometer is a weighted ball in a curved liquid-filled tube.

Radio Altimeter

The radio altimeter sends radio waves down from the aircraft and senses the time it takes for a wave to bounce back from the ground to the sensor and correlates that to height above the ground. Once within 2500 feet of the ground, the radio altimeter altitude displays in the lower right corner of the EADI. The radio altimeter displays changes in 50 foot increments above 1000 feet and 10 foot increments below 1000 feet. The drawing above shows a radio altimeter height of 840 feet above the ground.

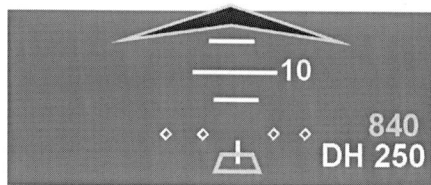

Decision Height Annunciation

The decision height on an approach can be displayed on the EADI by setting the appropriate height above touchdown with the "DH SET" button on the display select panel on the pedestal. The maximum decision height that can be set is 999 feet. The decision height digits flash when the aircraft is between DH + 50 feet and the selected DH. When the radio altimeter senses the aircraft has reached the decision height a yellow "DH" annunciator flashes for 5 seconds then becomes

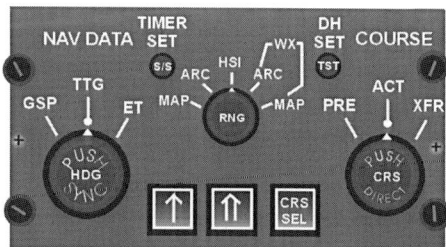

steady. When the radio altimeter senses the aircraft below 6 feet AGL, the annunciator automatically turns off and remains off until 100 feet above DH upon a missed approach or the next departure if the DH altitude is still set.

Marker Beacon Display

Marker beacon passage is annunciated in the upper right side of the EADI with a yellow box and OM for the outer marker, MM for the middle marker, and a hollow white box for an inner marker. All of the marker beacon annunciators flash when they are displayed.

Flight Control Mode Annunciation

The active or armed lateral and vertical Flight Control System (FCS) mode is displayed at the top of the EADI. An FCS mode is armed when selected on the flight director control panel and becomes active when the flight director captures the course. In addition to the display at the top of the EADI, annunciators on the top of the flight director control panel display which mode has been selected.

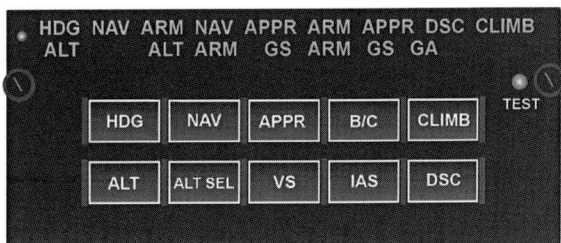

The lateral FCS modes are displayed in a single line on the left side of the EADI. The vertical FCS modes are shown in two lines on the right side of the instrument. The active FCS modes are displayed in green with the armed modes in white. When a new mode becomes active, it flashes for 5 seconds before coming steady.

The different lateral modes that can be displayed are GA (Go Around), LOC (Localizer), VOR, HDG (Heading), TEST, or blank if no lateral mode is selected. The different vertical modes that can be displayed are GA, GS (Glide Slope), ALTS (Altitude Preselect

Track), ALT ARM (Altitude Preselect Arm), ALT (Altitude), VS (Vertical Speed Hold Mode), IAS (Indicated Airspeed Hold Mode), CLM (Climb Mode), DSC (Descend Mode), or blank if no vertical mode is selected.

Autopilot/Yaw Damper Engage Status

When the autopilot is engaged, an AP/L (Autopilot Left) or AP/R (Autopilot Right) annunciator illuminates in the upper left side of the EADI. The L or R indicates which flight director control panel will operate the mode the autopilot is in. When the yaw damper is engaged, a YD annunciator illuminates one line below the autopilot engage annunciator.

When the autopilot is turned off by a pilot, the autopilot annunciator turns yellow and flashes for 5 seconds then turns white and remains steady. If a fault disengages the autopilot, the annunciator turns yellow and flashes until the pilot acknowledges it has turned off by pushing the disconnect button. When the pilot turns off the yaw damper the YD annunciator blanks. If a fault disengages the yaw damper, the annunciator turns yellow and flashes until the pilot acknowledges it has turned off, at which time the annunciator blanks.

Vertical Sync Status

With the flight director in the pitch (CLM or DSC) or vertical speed (VS) mode and the SYNC button pressed on the yoke, the flight director moves to match the current pitch or feet/minute of the aircraft. When the pitch sync is activated a yellow "SYNC" annunciator momentarily illuminates and overrides the trim message on the side (pilot or copilot) the sync button was pressed.

Trim Status

When the autopilot is on and the aileron, elevator, or rudder trim is mistrimmed, a yellow boxed annunciator flashes, alerting the pilot to the condition. A yellow boxed "A" indicates the aileron is mistrimmed, "E" indicates elevator trim, and "R" indicates rudder trim. The annunciator flashes for 5 seconds then goes steady when the mistrim occurs, with the

---

annunciation going blank once back in trim. If the out of trim condition gets excessive, the autopilot automatically disengages while in the out of trim condition.

Comparator Warnings

Each EADI compares pitch and roll data with the cross side EADI. When pitch or roll errors exceed 3 to 6 degrees, a boxed "PIT" or "ROL" annunciator illuminates, and a "COMPARE – PUSH TO RESET" annunciator flashes on the instrument panel.

Pushing the compare reset annunciator attempts to reset the system. If the annunciators remain off after reset, the system is working normally again. If the system still detects an error, the annunciator on the EADI remains illuminated and the annunciator on the instrument panel comes on again, but does not flash.

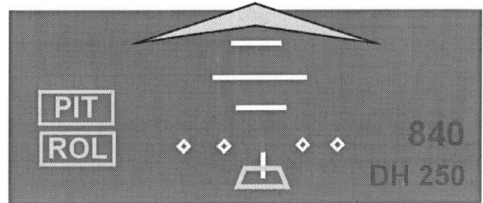

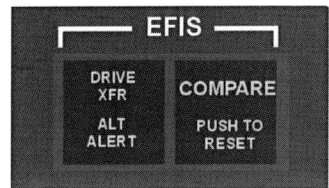

Warning Annunciators

There are 8 warning annunciators that illuminate when the EADI senses a failure within the unit or the data being provided to the unit. Each of the warning annunciators are red.

The attitude (ATT) annunciator indicates a failure of the attitude sensor. When the failure occurs, the pitch and roll scale, roll pointer, sky/ground display, and command bars disappear. The ATT annunciator flashes for 10 seconds then becomes steady.

The display processor unit (DPU) annunciator illuminates when the DPU fails. The non flashing DPU annunciator displays in large letters across the center of the EADI. If the annunciator remains illuminated for more than 5 seconds, the entire EADI display blanks except for the DPU

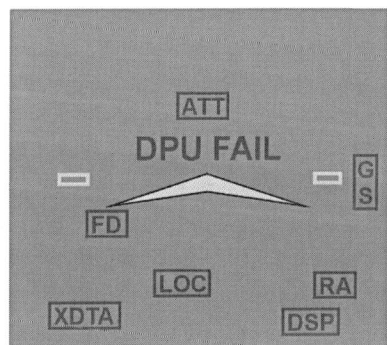

annunciator.

The glide slope (GS) annunciator illuminates and the glide slope scale and pointer disappear when a localizer frequency is selected and glide slope information is not being received or there is a failure in EADI glide slope display. The annunciator does not flash and remains illuminated until a glide slope is received or a VOR frequency is tuned in the nav radio.

When a failure in the radio altimeter is detected, a radio altimeter (RA) annunciator illuminates on the EADI. The annunciator flashes for 10 seconds then becomes steady. The DH set and DH annunciator display are also removed from view with a failure in the radio altimeter.

If a failure in the display select panel (DSP) occurs, the red annunciator illuminates in the lower right corner, replacing the DH set display. The annunciator flashes for 10 seconds then becomes steady. The lateral and vertical flight control mode annunciators along the top of the EADI disappear from view. The DH operates in the mode that was selected prior to the failure.

If the EADI detects no data or invalid data on the selected localizer (LOC), GPS, or VOR, the lateral deviation scale and pointer are removed from view and the appropriate lateral deviation fail annunciator illuminates above where the lateral deviation scale is usually displayed.

Each EADI compares data with each other and provides the comparator warnings when data differs. When the cross side data flow fails, a red "XDTA" annunciator flashes for 10 seconds then becomes steady in the lower left of the EADI.

If a failure occurs in the flight director system, the command bars disappear and an "FD" annunciator flashes for 10 seconds then becomes steady to the lower left of the aircraft display.

EFIS Test Button

On the EFIS power control panel, there are two EFIS test buttons, one for the pilot side and one for the copilot side. When the pilot side EFIS test button is pressed, the EADI should indicate 10° of additional pitch up and right roll, and 20° right heading change on the EHSI. A red "TEST" annunciator illuminates on the EADI. The comparator logic should also annunciate the ATT (EADI) and HDG (ESHI) comparator warning messages. When the copilot test button is pressed, the EADI should indicate 10° of additional pitch down and left roll, and 20° left heading change on the EHSI. The annunciators on the copilot side should be the same as described for the pilot side.

If either EFIS test buttons are held for longer than 4 seconds, the EFIS tubes blank, and all the warning annunciators associated with the EADI and EHSI illuminate.

EHSI

The EHSI can display data in three different formats; HSI (full compass rose), ARC (approach or sector), and MAP (enroute or map). These different formats are selected with the EHSI format switch on the display select panel shown here to the right.

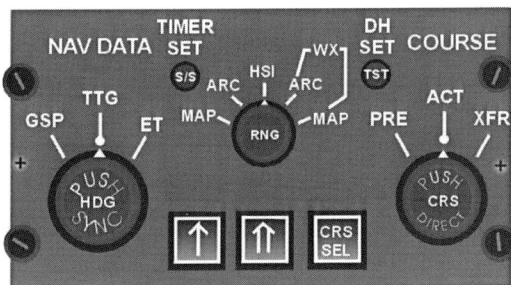

HSI Format

In the HSI format, a full compass rose is displayed similar to that of a conventional HSI. The EHSI adds additional situational awareness. It can display up to four courses on the same display, time to station, and ground speed.

Course Display

There are four courses that can be displayed on the EHSI. The active course is the green solid single bar course arrow. When the course switch on the display select panel is placed in the ACT position, the CRS SEL button to the left of the course switch scrolls through the different navigation course options. Repeatedly pressing and releasing the CRS SEL button steps through the available navigation sensors (VOR/LOC1, GPS, VOR/LOC2, LRN). The navigation sensor types are displayed on the left side of the EHSI (called the sensor annunciator).

Within 5 seconds of the desired navigation sensor being displayed, press and hold the CRS SEL button for at least ½ second to select that sensor as the active course arrow. If the CRS SEL button is held down for over ½ second before momentarily pressing and releasing it, the active course arrow automatically reverts to the on side VOR.

The secondary (preset) course is shown by the double blue dashed line course arrow on the EHSI. When the course switch on the display select panel is placed in the PRE position, the CRS SEL button scrolls through the navigation sensors for the preset course. The preset course sensor types are displayed below the active course annunciator on the left side of the EADI. The display on the EHSI shows whether the ACT or PRE course is selected with the switch by a round circle to the right of selected course sensor annunciation.

When the DME hold feature is used, an "H" annunciator illuminates below the selected course annunciator on the left side of the EADI.

When the display select panel course switch is moved to the course transfer (XFR) position, the preset course data is moved to the active course. The active

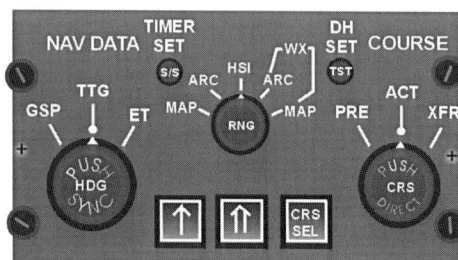

course moves to the preset position, but preset course arrow disappears. Setting the course switch to PRE and holding the CRS SEL button down for over ½ second can manually turn on the preset course arrow. The course switch is spring loaded to return to the ACT position after selecting XFR.

The two other courses that can be displayed on the EHSI are bearing pointers. Bearing pointers are like an RMI or ADF needle. The head of the needle points to the direct course to the station at all times. To turn on a bearing pointer, push the single or double arrow button just to the left of the CRS SEL button on the display select panel. Repeatedly pressing the bearing buttons steps through the navigation sensors that can be represented with the bearing pointer (VOR or ADF). Bearing pointer sensor selections are annunciated in the lower left of the EHSI for 5 seconds after a bearing pointer selection change. After 5

---

seconds they are removed from view. To turn off a bearing pointer, push and hold the respective bearing pointer button for over ½ second.

If the bearing pointer is on and a VOR is the sensor with a localizer frequency tuned, the bearing pointer automatically turns off.

Nav Data Display

The Nav Data button on the display select panel selects which display is shown in the upper right of the EHSI. The display can show groundspeed (GSP), time-to-go (TTG) or elapsed time (ET).

The elapsed time initializes at 00:00 on power up. It can be used to count up or count down. When pushing the TIMER SET S/S button, the timer starts to count up. The second press stops the timer and third resets it to zero. To have the counter count down, set the desired time to start from by rotating the TIMER SET knob. To start the count down, press the TIMER SET S/S button. After starting the timer, the groundspeed or time-to-go displays may be selected without disturbing the elapsed time count.

ARC Format

The arc format is a zoomed in view of the HSI format. It displays a 60 degree compass segment at the top of the display and the aircraft symbol in the bottom center. Most of the annunciators and features are the same as when the EHSI is in the HSI format. The exceptions are explained below.

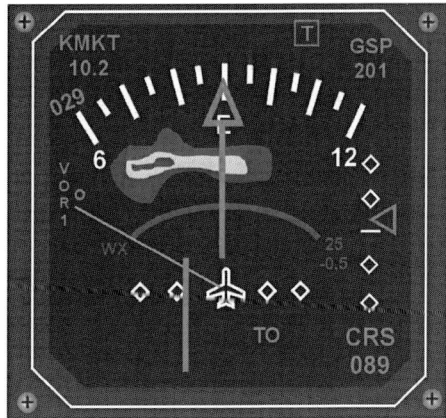

If the heading bug is moved to a heading not displayed in the 60 degree arc shown on the top of the EHSI, the heading cursor disappears and is replaced by a digital readout located in the upper right or left side of the display (shown as 029 in the display above). The digital readout display is on the side that is closest to the selected heading. A pink line extends out from the center of the aircraft symbol to the edge of the display at the selected heading angle.

One of the nicest features of the ARC format is that navaids can be displayed in the background of the display. Whatever is selected in the secondary (preset) course (VOR1, VOR2, LRN, or GPS) displays as a graphic in the background of the EHSI with the fix or navaid identifier. There is no course line or deviation bar displayed for the preset course in the ARC format. Bearing pointers can be displayed as they are in the HSI format.

The to/from arrow is replaced with the annunciator "TO" or "FR" below and to the right of the aircraft display on the ESHI.

The ring (RNG) knob on the display select panel selects how many miles are depicted on the EHSI. The dashed line running through the middle of the arc format EHSI is the half range arc. The number of miles that are depicted by the half range arc is annunciated below the right side of the arc. Turn the RNG knob to select ranges of 5, 10, 25, 50, 100, 200, 300, and 600 nm.

ARC/WX Format

Another feature of the ARC format is the ability to display weather radar. To add the weather radar display, turn the format switch on the display select panel to the ARC/WX position.

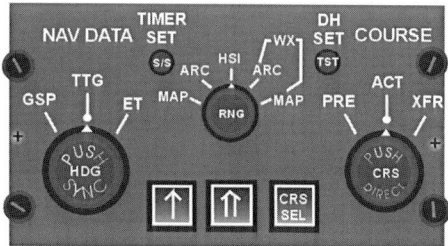

When the weather radar is displayed on the EHSI, the range is controlled on the weather radar panel rather than the RNG knob. The ranges that can be selected with weather radar displayed are 10, 25, 50, 100, or 300 nm.

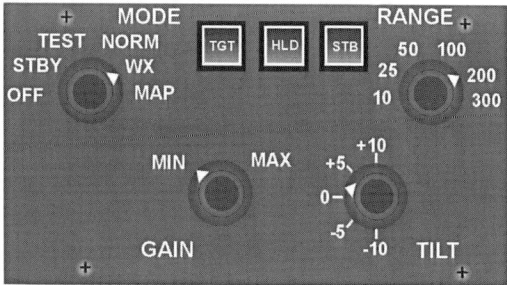

The MODE control switch on the weather radar control panel on the pedestal is used to select the different operating modes of the weather radar. The mode selected is annunciated on the left side of the half range arc on the

EHSI. The OFF mode turns the weather radar off. Selecting the STBY mode starts the radar on a 60 second warmup.

The TEST mode initiates a self-test of the radar system. Set the range to the 25 nm setting and a rainbow pattern of colored arcs display. The inner arc should be green and the arcs proceeding outward should be yellow, alternating red and magenta, yellow, and a green outer arc.

The weather (WX) mode turns on the weather detection of the radar. When precipitation is sensed, it is displayed on the EHSI in green, yellow, red, and magenta. The green represents the least intense precipitation, yellow the second level of precipitation intensity, red the third level, and magenta for the most intense precipitation. The black background indicates areas that precipitation is not detected. In the WX mode, automatic cyclic contour is turned on. When storm cells are detected, the red color is alternated with black to produce a slow flash to create emphasis.

The normal (NORM) mode also turns on the radar. It operates the same as the WX mode with the exception that the automatic cyclic contour feature is disabled.

The MAP mode uses the weather radar in a terrain mapping mode. The radar sends out radio waves and detects how many of these radio waves are sent back to the aircraft. The level of reflectivity is displayed as the different colors as explained above. The radar is not able to differentiate between precipitation and ground returns caused by terrain. The uniformity of the returns, tilt angle, and aircraft attitude and altitude can all be clues to the pilot whether it is precipitation or terrain that the radar is detecting. In the MAP mode, the automatic cyclic contour is disabled. Radar returns in the MAP mode are presented in cyan, yellow, or magenta (least to most reflective).

The GAIN control switch manually controls the gain of the radar. When set to maximum (MAX), the radar displays returns that exceed the Z1 reflectivity level (less than 20 dBz/less than .03 in/hr precipitation). As the gain is turned down towards minimum (MIN) the sensitivity of the radar is decreased so radar returns display as less intense.

The TILT control adjusts the pitch attitude of the radar antenna. It can be turned to adjust the antenna from +15 degrees to –15 degrees. As altitude and aircraft attitude is changed, you may necd to adjust the tilt to detect precipitation or ground returns.

There are three buttons labeled TGT, HLD, and STB between the mode and range knobs. The target (TGT) button activates the target alert feature. If the radar detects a return signal between 50 and 150 miles and +/- 15 degrees of current heading, a boxed "T" annunciator flashes in the upper right of the EHSI when in the ARC or HSI format. The annunciator is meant to alert the pilot to the possibility of significant weather ahead.

The hold (HLD) button freezes the radar display until the button is pressed again. This allows for detailed analysis of returns while the display is not updated. When the hold feature is used, it is annunciated on the EHSI to the left of the half arc display. The WX annunciator alternates with the HOLD annunciator.

The stabilization (STB) button turns on the radar antenna stabilization. This is normally left in the pushed in (on) position.

Map Format

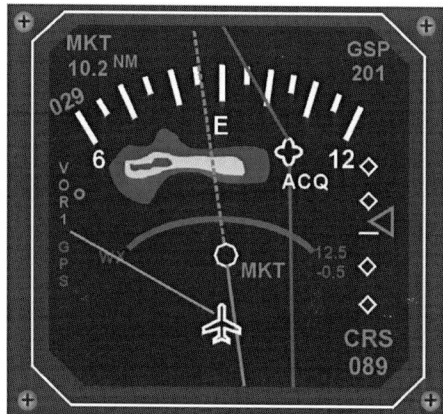

The MAP format of the EHSI is very similar to the ARC format. It displays a 60 degree compass segment at the top of the display and the aircraft symbol in the bottom center. Most of the annunciators and features are the same as when the EHSI is in the ARC format. The exceptions are explained below.

The course lines with the arrow and to/from annunciator have been removed in the MAP mode. The active course (VOR1 MKT in the display above) is displayed on the map with two green lines extending from it. When the active course is a VOR, an octagon shaped symbol is displayed on the map with respect to range and azimuth to the aircraft symbol. The selected course line displayed on the map is controlled by the course (CRS) knob on the display select panel. The solid green line indicates the course to the fix, and the dashed line is the course from the fix.

If a localizer frequency is selected or the DME hold feature is used, the VOR symbol, identifier, and course line are removed from the map. The sensor annunciator indicates "LOC" when the localizer frequency is selected. When DME hold is used, a yellow "H" annunciator displays to the right of the distance digits in the upper left of the EHSI, replacing the "NM" annunciator.

When the active course is a long range navigation (LNAV) sensor (GPS or Loran), multiple fixes can be displayed on the map. The fixes in the route programmed into the LNAV are displayed on the map with a solid line connecting each fix. Fixes are displayed as a open white cross, Tacans or VORTACs are displayed with the VORTAC symbol seen on a IFR or VFR chart, and airports are displayed as generic runway layout symbol.

The preset course display is similar to the active course display with the exception that the course line is blue instead of green. If the DME hold feature is used with the preset course the "H" annunciator displays below the sensor annunciator. A yellow "D" annunciator below the preset sensor annunciator indicates the DME has failed.

MAP/WX Format

The MAP/WX format adds weather radar to the map display. The features and operation of the weather radar are the same as when in the ARC/WX format explained above, with the exception that the target alert (TGT button and the yellow boxed "T" annunciator) feature is removed from the MAP format.

EHSI Warning Flags

There are 10 warning annunciators that can illuminate when the EHSI senses a failure within the unit or the data being provided to the unit.

If the navaid is not receiving DME or distance information from the LNAV, the distance digits and "NM" annunciator are replaced with a green dashed line. If there is a failure in the EHSI of reading the data, the dashed line disappears. Similar to the distance information, a dashed line replaces invalid ground speeds or time-to-go digits.

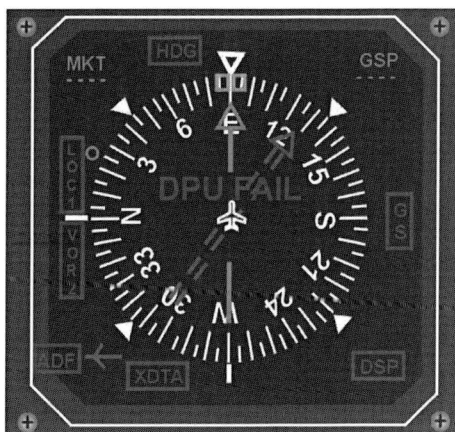

When there is a failure in the heading system or a discrepancy between the pilot and copilot side heading indications, a red boxed "HDG" annunciator illuminates in the upper left of the EHSI. The HDG annunciator flashes for 10 seconds then becomes steady.

The display processor unit (DPU) annunciator illuminates when the DPU fails. The non flashing DPU annunciator displays in large letters across the center of the EADI. If the annunciator remains illuminated for more than 5 seconds, the EADI display blanks, except for the DPU annunciator.

The glide slope (GS) annunciator illuminates, and the glide slope scale and pointer disappear when a localizer frequency is selected and glide slope information is not being received or there is a failure in EHSI glide slope display. The annunciator does not flash and remains illuminated until a glide slope is received or a VOR frequency is tuned in the nav radio.

If a failure in the display select panel (DSP) occurs, the red annunciator illuminates in the lower right corner. The annunciator flashes for 10 seconds then becomes steady. The EHSI continues to operate in the mode it was prior to the DSP failure.

Each EHSI compares data with each other and provides the comparator warnings when data differs. When the cross side data flow fails, a red "XDTA" annunciator flashes for 10 seconds then becomes steady in the lower left of the EADI. Any display driven by the cross data is also flagged.

If a bearing pointer sensor fails or the navaid is not received, the sensor annunciator becomes red and boxed. The bearing pointer on the EHSI also disappears.

If a navigation sensor failure is detected or the navaid is not received, the active or preset course sensor annunciator becomes boxed and red. The deviation bar is centered and the to/from display is removed from view. If in the MAP or ARC mode, the navaid symbol and connecting lines are removed from view.

Reversionary Panel

The reversionary panel for the EFIS system is located on the pedestal. The reversionary panel allows the pilot to select backup inputs to the EFIS system or display a composite of both the EADI and EHSI information on one tube. The reversionary panel is slightly different for aircraft not equipped with an autopilot.

The AP/L AP/R switch transfers the autopilot from the pilot side (AP/L) to the copilot side (AP/R). When transferred, the flight director panel on the copilot side controls which mode the autopilot controls the aircraft in.

The ADC TEST button tests the air data computer for proper operation. If any faults are sensed, the appropriate annunciator illuminates on the EFIS system.

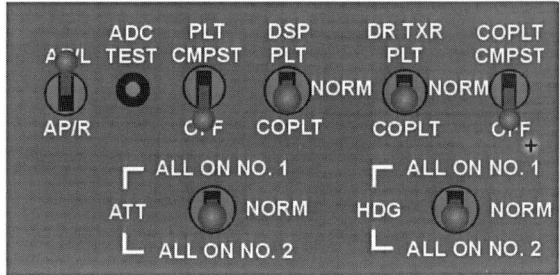

The PLT CMPST or COPLT CMPST switches display a composite of both the EADI and EHSI information on both of the tubes on that side. This could be used if one of the tubes failed.

The DSP PLT/NORM/COPLT switch is usually in the NORM center position, which will have the pilot and copilot use their own display select panel (DSP) to control the EFIS system. If the switch is placed in the DSP PLT position, the format the pilot selects on the DSP on the left side controls the EFIS system on both sides. When the switch is in the COPLT position, the right DSP controls the display on both sides.

The DR XFR PLT/NORM/COPLT switch is also in the NORM position for normal operations. When placed in the PLT or COPLT position, the EFIS uses the drive unit from the side selected to run the EFIS on both sides.

The bottom row of switches controls the attitude (ATT) and heading (HDG) systems. In the normal (NORM) mode, each sides EFIS system uses its own attitude and heading systems. When placed in ALL ON NO. 1 or 2, both side EFIS systems use a single side attitude or heading information.

EFIS Auxilary Power

An EFIS auxiliary power system is installed to prevent the EFIS system from losing power during an airstart. It is not meant to power the EFIS system should the aircraft lose electrical power. The auxiliary battery is only powerful enough to operate the EFIS system for a short period of time, like when a drop in

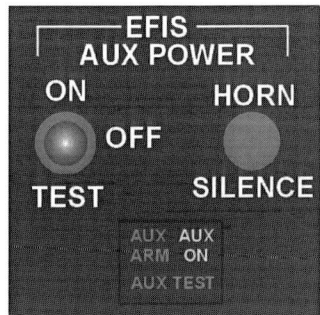

voltage occurs during an airstart. The auxiliary battery is located in the nose avionics compartment.

The control panel for the auxiliary power is on the lower left of the instrument panel. With the EFIS aux power switch on, the avionics master switch on, and the EFIS display being powered by the left generator bus, the green AUX ARM annunciator illuminates. If voltage to the EFIS displays drops below 18 volts, the yellow AUX ON annunciator illuminates along with a beeping warning horn. Silence the horn by pressing the horn silence button next to the EFIS Aux Power switch. The horn beeps and the AUX ON annunciator illuminates during shutdown if the avionics master switch is turned off before the EFIS aux power switch is turned off.

To test the auxiliary battery, hold the EFIS aux power switch to the test position until the AUX TEST annunciator illuminates. If the AUX TEST annunciator does not illuminate (even momentarily) within 5 seconds of holding the switch to the test position, consult with maintenance.

With the EFIS aux power switch on, the auxiliary battery is not connected to the EFIS system until the left squat switch senses the aircraft in the air. This prevents the auxiliary battery from powering the EFIS system while on the ground. The auxiliary battery is continuously charged by the left generator bus.

Notes:

Appendix A
GOVERNORS

Governors can be used to maintain constant speed in propellers and engines, as well as provide metered amounts of fuel to the engine. Most governors are of similar design using flyweights, speeder springs, and a pilot valve. This section discusses an oil "pressure to decrease pitch" constant speed, fully feathering propeller governor; yet its principles can apply to many governor operations in any aircraft.

Constant speed is the ability to set a propeller to a specific rpm and to maintain that while airspeed and power may vary. Rpm is controlled by varying the pitch of the propeller blades. As propeller blade angle is reduced, the torque required to turn the propeller is also reduced (because of the reduced airflow the blade has to displace). If everything else remains constant, the rpm of the propeller will increase. If the propeller blade angle is increased, the required torque increases, and the blade will slow down. Therefore, by varying the blade angle or pitch of the propeller, you can control the rpm.

The pitch of the propeller blades is controlled hydraulically by engine oil. The oil is pumped into the propeller hub on the forward side of a piston, which is attached to the propeller blades. As oil pressure increases, the piston moves aft, rotating the propeller blades to a reduced pitch.

To oppose the force of oil (trying to increase the pitch of the propeller blades) there are counterweights and a large spring. The aerodynamic twisting force of the propeller also opposes the force of oil but works independent of the governor.

On the opposite side of the piston there is a large spring that opposes oil pressure. Counterweights are rectangular weights attached to the base of the propeller blades. They are mounted at about a 45° angle to the blade. As the blade rotates around, centrifugal force tries to pull the counterweights into the plane of rotation. This attempts to increase the pitch of the propeller. The aerodynamic twisting force of the blade is based on the fact that it is shaped like a wing and wants to rotate into the relative wind. Normal cruise blade angle is 30° to 45°. As wind hits the bottom of the blade (wing) the force is to decrease the blade angle of the propeller. When the opposing forces are equal, oil flow to the propeller stops, causing the piston to stop also.

Pitch is increased by moving oil out of the propeller hub. When oil pressure decreases in the hub, the piston moves forward, and the propeller blades move toward high pitch (feather). The piston moves forward until opposing forces are equal. If all the oil flows out of the propeller, the piston will move all the way forward and the propellers will feather. This happens when the propeller lever in the cockpit is moved to the feather position or if all oil pressure is lost.

The propeller governor is geared by and mounted on the engine. The power from the engine runs an oil gear pump and a set of flyweights. The gear pump boosts oil pressure to 750 psi to provide quick and positive response by the propeller. The rotational speed of the flyweight assembly varies directly with engine speed. The flyweights are L-shaped and show response to two forces; engine speed and a speeder spring. As the engine speeds up, so do the flyweights. As the flyweights speed up, centrifugal force tends to spin them outward and upward. Opposing this force is a speeder spring. The spring can increase or decrease the tension on the base of the flyweights. As tension increases it takes a greater force to spin the flyweights upward and outward.

The flyweights are connected to a pilot valve. As the flyweights move upward and outward, the pilot valve raises. When the flyweights slow down or tension gets increased and they move inward and down, the pilot valve lowers. The pilot valve, depending on its position, directs the flow of oil either to or from the propeller hub. As the pilot valve raises, oil is allowed to flow from the propeller hub back to the engine sump. As the pilot valve lowers, oil is sent from the gear pump to the propeller hub.

The propeller lever in the cockpit is connected to the speeder spring in the governor. When the propeller lever is pulled back (requesting a slower propeller rpm) the compression on the speeder spring reduces, allowing the flyweights to spin upward and outward more easily. The pilot valve also raises more easily, allowing oil to flow from the propeller hub back to the engine oil sump. This increases the pitch of the propeller, which slows the blades down.

When the propeller lever in the cockpit is set and everything remains constant, you have an on-speed condition. The speeder spring and engine speed are set, all forces are equal, and oil is not flowing to or from the propeller hub. If you begin a descent and the airspeed starts to increase, the propellers will momentarily start to speed up. The governor will sense this overspeed condition because the engine will speed up. This will cause the flyweights to spin outward and upward (due to the additional speed and centrifugal force) which will raise the pilot valve, allowing oil to flow from the propeller hub back to the engine sump. Oil pressure will decrease, and blade angle will increase, which puts the propellers back on speed. The scenario above happens in a fraction of a second.

If speed is reduced in a descent, the propellers will start to slow due to the reduced airflow. The primary governor will sense the underspeed condition by a slowing of engine speed. This will slow the flyweights moving them inward and downward, which lowers the pilot valve moving oil to the propeller hub. As oil pressure increases blade angle decreases, returning the propellers to an on-speed condition.

Notes:

Appendix B
DEFINITIONS

Abifricated Plenum .... Wire mesh screen that air passes through to keep FOD out of the engine.

ACM Bypass .... By positioning a valve through the temperature dial, airflow bypasses the ACM so the air does not get cooled.

Advisory Annunciator .... Green or white light in the cockpit telling the pilot the status of an item (on or off).

Annunciator .... Light in the cockpit advising the crew of the status of an item.

Anti-ice .... Equipment designed to prevent the formation of ice on the aircraft.

Aux Transfer Switches ... Allows fuel to be transferred from the auxiliary tanks to the main tank.

Axial Flow .... Airflow that is directed in a straight line.

Beta .... Propeller blade angle range (from +7° to -3°) that produces less thrust than idle. Used in taxi to reduce speed without the use of brakes, it can be reached by having the power levers at idle and lifting them up over the detent.

Bleed Air Valve .... Valve used to control airflow from the engine used in the environmental system.

Burner Can .... The location in the engine where compressed air, fuel and a spark meet to create a controlled explosion.

Bus .... Distribution point for electricity.

Caution Annunciator ...... Yellow light in the cockpit that indicates a malfunction where there is a checklist procedure that needs to be accomplished.

Cavitation .... High pressure fluid in motion that forms vapor pockets of air around the source of pressure causing a loss of efficiency.

Centrifugal Flow .... Airflow that is directed at a 90° angle from where it entered.

DEFINITIONS   151

Challenge/Response....... The recommended procedure to use a checklist in a multi-pilot crew. The non-flying pilot reads the item on the checklist and the flying pilot makes the response.

Compressor Stall............ A back flow of air. Causes a non laminar flow over the turbine blades causing them to stall (like a wing would). It makes a loud banging sound.

Condition Lever .... Sets idle speed of the engine and is a fuel shutoff valve.

Critical Phase of Flight . Portions of a flight that require undivided pilot attention including taxi, takeoff, departure climb, approach and landing.

CT Wheel........................ Another name for the compressor turbine. It absorbs 60% of the energy coming from the burner can to power the gas generator section of the engine.

Current Limiter.............. A fuse that senses a specific amount of heat to blow, not allowing current to flow through it. It is a way for the electrical system to isolate part of the system during a malfunction.

Datum .... The point where all weights are measured from for weight and balance purposes.

De-ice............................ Equipment designed to remove ice from the aircraft after it has already formed.

Diffuser Tube .... Like a stator vane but they direct airflow in a specific direction rather than in the most efficient direction. Used for getting airflow to encompass the burner can.

Diode............................. One way valve for electricity. Allows current to flow only in one direction.

Drag Brace .... The rigid component of the gear when it is down. It is a two piece metal bar that is hinged in the middle and locks in the overcenter position.

EFIS.............................. Electronic Flight Instrumentation System. Flight and performance information is displayed on cathode-ray tubes or flat-panel liquid-crystal display.

Ejector........................... Air control unit that cools the temperature of the air passing through it.

EVA Tubing.................... Plastic type of tubing wrapped around all bleed air lines. It will illuminate a warning annunciator in the cockpit if melted by a bleed air line rupture.

Firewall Fuel Valves...... Fuel shutoff valves that are located in the wing.

Flyweights ⠀⠀⠀⠀⠀⠀⠀ L-shaped weights connected to a rotating shaft. As the shaft speeds up, the flyweights rotate upward and outward.

Gas Generator .... The aft section of the engine that is used to compress air.

Hot Battery Bus.............. Electrical bus that is connected directly to the battery. Those items receive power whether the battery switch is on or off.

Hot Start........................ Malfunction during the start process that causes ITT to raise rapidly beyond its limitations.

Hung Start...................... Malfunction of the secondary fuel nozzles that cause N_1 to hang at 36 to 39% during the start process.

Ice Vane .... Metal plate that extends downward in the engine air inlet to deflect ice and other particles heavier than air from being digested by the engine.

Inverter.......................... Turns DC power from the battery or generators into AC power.

Line Contractor.............. Bridge in the electrical system that allows current from the generators to be connected to the rest of the electrical system.

Master Caution Flasher. Yellow light in the cockpit that flashes anytime a caution annunciator illuminates.

Master Warning Flasher Red light in the cockpit that flashes anytime a warning annunciator illuminates.

Mode Controller .... Dial on the copilot's left subpanel used to control cabin temperature.

P₃ Purge Tank................ Tank of pressurized air that releases itself into the fuel lines in the engine when fuel pressure drops below 100 psi. This burns off residual fuel in the engine when shut down.

Power Turbine............... Turbine used to create thrust. In a turboprop they are directly linked to the propellers.

Pressure Vessel.............. The part of the aircraft that is pressurized by engine bleed air.

Red Light Item................ Any malfunction that causes a red annunciator to illuminate in the cockpit.

Reduction Gear Box....... Takes high speed, low energy torque from a rotating shaft and turns it into a low speed, high energy torque.

Relay .... Automatic device that reacts to a current or voltage change by activating a switch in an electric circuit.

Reverse.......................... The lowest range of the power levers. Produces a negative blade angle on the propellers and increases engine speed to get reverse thrust from the propellers.

Scavenge Oil Pump....... Pump used to return oil to the engine oil sump.

Speeder Spring............... Sets tension on the flyweights in a governor.

Stabilons........................ Horizontal flight surface located below the T-tail. It acts as an additional wing producing greater pitch stability.

Standby Pumps   Backup fuel boost pump used for fuel cross transfer and in the event of an engine driven boost pump failure.

Stator Vane .... Series of metal pieces that direct airflow from one stage of compression to the next in the most efficient manner so energy loss is at a minimum.

Switch............................ We have limited control over a switch in the electrical system. It can open automatically or manually, but it must be closed manually.

Tailets   Vertical fins that extend downward from the horizontal stabilizer. They aid in directional stability.

T-Handle .... Fuel shutoff valve located on the instrument panel. It is a clear handle shaped like a T.

Ties.................................. The aircraft electrical system has control over a tie to close and open it during normal operations.

Torque Meter .... Reads engine speed in foot/lbs.

Turbine.......................... Fan-shaped blades set in a circular pattern.

Vent Blower.................... Fan used to direct airflow into the cabin.

Vortex Generators.......... Direct airflow to decrease drag or to keep a laminar flow over the wing.

Warning Annunciator   Red light in the cockpit noting a malfunction that needs immediate attention by memory by the pilot.

Notes:

Appendix C
ABBREVIATIONS

AC	Alternating Current
ACM	Air Cycle Machine
AFM	Airplane Flight Manual
AFX	Autofeather
ALT	Altitude
ANN	Annunciator
A/P	Autopilot
AUX	Auxiliary
BAT	Battery
BK	Brake
BL	Bleed (air)
COL	Collector
CT	Compressor Turbine
DC	Direct Current
DI	De-ice
DIFF	Differential
EFIS	Electronic Flight Instrumentation System
EMER	Emergency
ENG	Engine
ENGA	Engage
ENVIR	Environmental
EVA	Ethylene Vinyl Acetate
FOD	Foreign Object Damage
FP	Flying Pilot
FW	Firewall
GEN	Generator

HED	Hall Effect Device
HI	High
INBD	Inboard
ITT	Interstage Turbine Temperature
KIAS	Knots Indicated Airspeed
L	Left
LO	Low
MAN	Manual
M_{MO}	Maximum Mach Operating speed
N_1	Gas generator speed in percent of maximum
N_2	Propeller rpm
NFP	Non-Flying Pilot
NiCad	Nickel Cadium Battery
OUTBD	Outboard
OVHT	Overheat
$P_{2.5}$	Engine station 2.5
P_3 *air*	Bleed air taken from engine station 3
POH	Pilots operating handbook
PT6	Pratt and Whitney's sixth generation of turboprop engines
PWR	Power
QTY	Quantity
R	Right
RB	Rudder Boost
RDR	Rudder
T_5	Engine station 5
V_1	Takeoff decision speed
V_2	Takeoff safety speed
VCM	Vapor Cycle Machine
V_{LE}	Landing gear extended speed

V_{LO}	Landing gear operation speed
V_{mc}	Minimum Control speed
V_{MO}	Maximum operating speed in knots
V_R	Rotation speed
V_{REF}	Reference speed for landing
WG	Wing
XFR	Transfer
YD	Yaw Damp

Notes:

ABBREVIATIONS

Appendix D
EFFICIENCY

In Chapter 2 Engines, you learned that only 25% of the compressed air supports the combustion in the engine. 60% of that 25% is used to power the gas generator section of the engine, which leaves only 40% of that 25% (10% overall) of air to turn the propeller. On the surface, using only 25% of the available air sounds inefficient. What happened to the other 75% of the air?

The ITT is measured inside the burner can where the 25% of the air mixes with fuel to create combustion. ITT in cruise generally runs up to 720° Celsius with a limitation on start to go up to 1000° C. There are not many metals that can withstand that type of heat, especially when you consider trying to conserve weight. That is where the 75% of the air that does not support combustion comes in.

Consider this example. Imagine putting a candle in an empty coffee can. The flame from the candle needs oxygen to burn, so if the lid were put on the coffee can the flame would extinguish. If a hole was put in the side of the coffee can and the lid placed on it, the candle would still burn but the flame would angle toward the hole. This creates a hot spot next to the hole in the can. Over time that area of the can will deteriorate faster than the rest of the can due to the heat. Now imagine putting small pin sized holes on every side of the can. Where would the flame burn now? Yes, right in the center of the can, without creating any hot spots.

The burner can in the engine is the same as the coffee can in the example. It has hundreds of small pin-sized holes where air flows into it. The 75% of the air that does not support combustion is used to center the flame and keep the 700° C temperatures away from the metal exterior of the burner can. So what sounded like inefficiency is actually put to good use, allowing lighter weight materials to be used in the engine construction.

The fact that only 40% of the energy of the air coming out of the combustion chamber is used to turn the propeller is not an inefficiency either. The remaining 60% of the energy is used to create a self-sustaining cycle to keep the engine running. The CT wheel (that absorbs the 60% of the energy) is connected to the same shaft as the five compressors. When the engine is being started, there is little airflow going through it. As 60% of the energy of this airflow gets used by the

CT, it begins to turn the five compressors faster. As the five compressors start turning faster they compress more air. As more air gets compressed, the CT uses the more energy to turn the five compressors even faster. The cycle continues and continues, so the more air the CT uses the more air the compressors have to compress.

To control the cycle of compressing air to maintain the engine speed you want, the power levers meter fuel to the burner can through the use of a governor. The fuel flow governor has many of the same properties of a basic propeller governor. (See appendix A for a review of governor operation.) If the gas generator section starts to run faster than you have selected with the power lever, the pilot valve raises, decreasing the fuel flow to the burner can. Less fuel = less combustion = slower gas generator speed.

Therefore, what appeared to be major inefficiencies with the engine really are important parts of their operation. The only real inefficiency the engine has is it loses 3.6% of its energy having the reverse flow design and the engine split at the T_5 station. The reverse flow design does decrease the overall engine size and weight, and the engine split reduces maintenance costs; so it is a trade off.

Index

C

cabin
  pressurization
    bumps • 81
    controller • 79
    switch • 80–81
    temperature control • 82–83
    switch • 83
cabin briefer • 128
CABIN DOOR
  annunciator • 4
cable, fire, specifications • 32
CARGO DOOR
  annunciator • 5
caution
  master flasher
    canceling • 30
caution annunciator
  defined • 151
  lights • 29
cavitation • 94, 151
centrifugal flow • 151
centrifugal flow compressor • 13–14
challenge/response method • 152
checklist
  airstair door security • 4–5
cockpit
  overview • 2
  temperature control • 83–84
components, of landing gear • 67–68
compressor
  axial flow • 13–14
compressor centrifugal flow • 13–14
compressor stall • 152
compressor turbine • 15
condition lever
  defined • 152
  fuel shut off valve • 93
constant speed governor • 147
continuous cable loop • 32
control amplifier • 32
controller, pressurization, operation of • 81
controls
  engine

power levers • 18
critical phase of flight • 152
cross transfer
  fuel • 95–96
  procedure for • 96
CT wheel • 152
current limiter • 152
  defined • 55
  schematic symbol • 55

D

datum • 152
DC GEN
  annunciator • 59
de-ice • 101, 152
  brake
    bleed air • 77
de-ice boot • 107, 108
  on T-tail • 6
  propeller • 109
de-ice systems • *See also individual system names*
  propeller de-ice • 109–10
detector, battery charge current • 58
diffuser tube • 152
diode
  defined • 55, 152
  schematic symbol • 55
distribution, electrical system • 60
door
  airstair
    opening • 4
    overview • 3–5
    pressure seal • 4
    safety features of • 5
    security checklist • 4–5
  emergency exit
    opening • 7
  emergency exits • 7
drag brace • 67, 152
drag, parasite • 46
drains, fuel • 96–97

E

EADI • 129

F

I

ice accumulation, prevention of • 102
ice protection
    types of • 101. *See also individual types*
        anti-ice • 101
        de-ice • 101
ice vane
    air inlet • 104–6
    defined • 153
IGNITION ON
    annunciator • 25, 26
inertial separators • *See air inlet ice vanes*
interstage turbine temperature • 12
inverter
    defined • 153
    overview • 63–64
ITT • 15, 19, 161
ITT gauge • 20

J

jiffy pop fuse • *See current limiter*

L

landing gear
    annunciator
        HYD FLUID LOW • 70
    components of • 67–68
    handle • 69
        "DOWN" position • 70
        "UP" position • 70
    hydraulic
        extension • 69–70
        retraction • 69–70
    hydraulic fill can • 87
    main gear • 69
    nose gear • 68
    overview • 67
    position indicators • 70–71
    power levers for, warning horn • 71
    warning horn • 71
lever

power • 18
propeller • 50–51
light polarizing • 3
limitations
    airspeed • 8
    airspeed indicator • 9
    generator • 64
line contactor
    defined • 56, 153
    schematic symbol • 56
low pitch stop • 46
    propeller governors • 46–47
low pitch, testing • 50

M

magnetic compass, windshield heat affect on • 102
main gear • 69
maintenance, fuel shut off valve • 94
MAN STEER FAIL
    annunciator • 74
MAN TIES CLOSE
    annunciator • 62
master caution flasher
    canceling • 30
    defined • 153
master warning flasher • 29–30
    defined • 153
mixing plenum • 85
mode controller • 153

N

NESA • *See non-electrostatic application*
NiCad battery
    advantages of • 57
    defined • 57
    disadvantages of • 58
    overview • 57–58
    schematic symbol • 57
    switch for • 57
Nickel Cadium Battery • *See NiCad battery*
noise, cabin, reducing • 53

non-electrostatic application • 102, 107
nose gear • 68
nose section • 1–2

O

oil cooler • 24
oil pressure gauge • 21–22
oil temperature gauge • 21–22
oil-to-fuel heat exchangers • 106
outflow valve • 80
overspeed governor • 48
   propeller speed maintained by • 46
   testing • 49
oxygen mask
   in cockpit • 2
   in passenger cabin • 3

P

P test • 84
P3 • *See bleed air*
P3 air • 12
P3 purge tank • 154
parasite drag • 46
passenger cabin
   emergency exit
      opening • 7
   emergency exits • 7
   overview • 2–3
PITCH TRIM OFF
   annunciator • 40
pitot heat • 103
PITOT HEAT
   annunciator • 103
plenum, mixing • 85
pneumatic pressure • 86–87
pneumatic pressure gauge • 108
poppet valve • 80
position indicators
   landing gear • 70–71
power levers • 18
   alpha range • 50
   beta range • *18*, 50
   idle range • *18*
   landing gear

warning horn • 71
   regions • 18
   reverse range • *18*, 50
power turbine • 154
pressure
   pneumatic • 86–87
pressure vessel • 78, 80
   defined • 154
pressurization • 78–79
   altitude warning • 81
   bumps • 81
   cabin pressure switch • 80–81
   controller, operation of • 81
   limits • 84
   outflow valve • 80
   poppet valve • 80
primary flight controls
   aileron • 39
   elevator • 39
primary governor • 46–48
   backup for • 48
   beta valve • 47–48
   propeller speed maintained by • 46
prist • 97, 106
propeller
   blade angle • 46
   low pitch stop • 46
   overview • 45
   pre-takeoff tests
      low pitch • 50
      overspeed governor • 49
      primary governor • 49–50
propeller de-ice • 109–10
   manual • 109
propeller de-ice boot • 109
propeller governor, test • 49–50
propeller governors • *See also*
   individual governor names
   low pitch stop • 46–47
   overview • 46
   primary • 46–48
propeller hub • 47
propeller levers • 50–51
propeller range • 19
propeller tachometer • 20–21
pump
   boost • 93, 94
purge tank • 94
PWR STEER ENGA
   annunciator • 73

PWR STEER FAIL
annunciator • 74

X

XFR VALVE FAIL
annunciator • 96

Y

yaw damp • 40, 42
YD RB FAIL
annunciator • 42